CW01513106

MERCHANDISE FOR AUTHORS

ENGAGE YOUR READERS
WHILE INCREASING YOUR INCOME

MELISSA ADDEY

Merchandise for Authors
Copyright © 2016 by Melissa Addey. All rights reserved.
First Print Edition: October 2016

First Paperback Print Edition: 2016 in United Kingdom

Published by Letterpress Publishing

Cover and Formatting: Streetlight Graphics

Epub: 978-1-910940-40-2
Kindle: 978-1-910940-38-9
Paperback: 978-1-910940-39-6 and 978-1-910940-42-6

No part of this book may be reproduced, scanned, or distributed in any printed or electronic form without permission. Please do not participate in or encourage piracy of copyrighted materials in violation of the author's rights. Thank you for respecting the hard work of this author.

Although every precaution has been taken in the preparation of this book, the publisher and author assume no responsibility for errors or omissions. Neither is any liability assumed for damages resulting from the use of this information contained herein.

CONTENTS

About Melissa

I grew up on an organic farm in Umbria, Italy and was home-educated until I went to university in London aged 19.

Along the way I worked for Sainsbury's Head Office developing new products and packaging; for Roehampton University, mentoring student entrepreneurs; I undertook a Master's degree focused on innovation; and worked as a business consultant offering mentoring and Government grants to entrepreneurs.

I now live in London with my husband and two children, looking after the kids and writing. I write historical novels as well as non-fiction books and articles for magazines. In the autumn of 2016 I'll be starting a Ph.D. in Creative Writing at the University of Surrey.

Do visit and contact me at www.melissaaddey.com
Facebook: MelissaAddeyAuthor
Pinterest: MelissaAddey
Twitter: @MelissaAddey

OTHER BOOKS BY MELISSA:

Historical fiction:
The Consorts, 2016 (a free e-Book
on my website), Letterpress
The Fragrant Concubine, 2015, Letterpress

Non-fiction:
The Happy Commuter, 2016, Letterpress
The Storytelling Entrepreneur, 2016, Letterpress
100 Things to do while Breastfeeding, 2015
(also an audiobook), Letterpress

For the 10k group and their entrepreneurial mindset

Foreword

This is a really valuable resource. Melissa has clearly used the time she spent with the British Library to good effect, giving excellent advice to the many writers with whom she worked, and has now generously shared her thoughts in a format that means a much wider audience can benefit. While I both learnt a lot and received much further food for thought, there are three things I would like to emphasise before you start thinking about how you too can get involved in creating merchandise around your writing.

The first is a reminder of why you should bother. When writers want to write, why should they spend time thinking about converting their themes and ideas into other saleable materials?

Because readers who like a particular style of writing are generally curious about who provided it. It follows that they may want to invest more significantly in the author's view of the world.

Of course their next book may be the preferred option, but in the meantime they may be keen to adopt or display other ideas that come from the same mind.

When life was simpler for writers, they wrote and readers admired them from afar (or through a respectful letter to their publishers), and it was possible for them to maintain a lofty independence from their market. Today, it's very hard for a writer to insist that their book 'says it all'; the role of the author is, increasingly, to get out and promote their work, perhaps through literary festivals, involvement in social media or giving talks to organisations likely to be interested. It follows that having a range of additional materials related to your work can extend the relationship created, and not only enable your readers to feel more loyal to you, but allow them to promote their enthusiasm to others. This benefits all parties, from publishers and booksellers who invest in your work, to new readers who may see the marketing materials and be tempted to find out what all the fuss is about.

The second is that today's reader generally takes care to validate their choice of reading material. With the general decline of the printed press and reduced space given to book reviews (because they don't attract much advertising), there are a variety of means for attracting readers' attention, and together these enable the reinforcement of an author's brand. Readers no longer rely on being told what to read; today they look for evidence that a particular author is worth the investment of their time and money (and the former may be more significant than the latter). It follows that being seen to take yourself seriously, and inclined to intrigue your market by offering a range of related goods, may not only extend the range of 'touch points' through which existing readers hear about your work, but attract the attention of a wider audience, making them more likely to give new work a trial.

My third and final point is that peripheral activity of the kind Melissa describes should never replace the time and effort put into creating content worth reading. While it's a good idea to think about what kind of resources could be developed – and this can be pondered while you are writing – I thoroughly endorse her commitment to produce items that affirm the value and ethic of the central content and extend the relationship with the reader, rather than creating additional branded material for its own sake – or producing it too early in the process, before you have finalised the feel of your manuscript. Readers are not going to be impressed by add-on materials if the basic product is not one with which they wish to be associated. The same goes for her emphasis on ensuring that the materials you create affirm the core qualities of your brand, and that you are producing a product that you yourself would want to buy.

Melissa talks about the importance of encouragement and, in particular, the value of cheerleaders. I am one of hers. I am endlessly impressed by her lively mind, her energy, the quality of her ideas and her ongoing generosity. As with all her other endeavours, I consistently wish her well – and advise you to take her advice.

Dr Alison Baverstock

Associate Professor of Publishing, Kingston University

THE BRITISH LIBRARY'S BUSINESS & IP CENTRE

This book has been written in collaboration with the British Library's Business & IP Centre, and was generously funded by The Leverhulme Trust through their Artist in Residence grants scheme which seeks to foster creative collaboration between artists and host institutions.

The Business & IP Centre at the British Library supports entrepreneurs from all walks of life to start and grow successful businesses. The Centre provides access to the UK's largest collection of business and intellectual property data alongside training, expertise and networks in a trusted and inspiring space, supporting thousands of entrepreneurs and small business owners each year.

The Artist in Residence project has enabled users of the Centre to explore the application of creative writing and narrative techniques as business strategies, actively raising awareness of the fruitful connections between business, creativity and storytelling in both practical and theoretical ways. The residency has also developed con-nections between the Library's business audiences and other areas of collection specialism, increasing oppor-tunities for inter-disciplinary research and encouraging business users to be inspired by the unique items held in the Library's vast collection.

Thanks must go to The Leverhulme Trust for their support of this project, and in addition to the business owners, authors and entrepreneurs who have engaged with the project through attending workshops and one-to-ones and generously sharing their stories and experiences.

The Leverhulme Trust

**Business &
IP Centre**
London

Acknowledgements

I would like to say a huge thank you to the Leverhulme Trust for their funding, and the British Library's Business & IP Centre for hosting the position of Writer in Residence. It has been the most extraordinary gift of a year: I have had so much fun, done so many wonderful things and met so many great people through this role. Thank you to Noelle, who built up my relationship with the British Library from the beginning, and a very big thank you to Jess, who said 'yes' and followed the whole thing through. We did it!

Thank you to all the authors who answered lots of questions and allowed me to use their products as examples of merchandise for this book. Your stories are inspiring.

To the many writers who attended my workshops in the Business and IP Centre at the British Library, thank you. Your ideas, discussions and questions gave me new material for this book and I hope you will all develop great merchandise of your very own. Don't forget to write and tell me about it!

A humble thank you to Alison, who always gives more than I would dare to ask for!

Grateful thanks to Gale at Winskill Editorial who gave both polish and insight to the manuscript. And to Streetlight Graphics: you are the best. Couldn't do it without you.

Thank you to Ryan, who always makes things possible, and to Seth and Isabelle for letting Mummy work 'in the library'.

To everyone who said 'Wow!' when I told them about this residency… you were absolutely right.

1. Introduction

I spent over fifteen years in business, mostly developing new products and packaging, as well as mentoring entrepreneurs at all levels, from students to established business owners. I have a lot of interest in innovation and creativity, in which I did a Master's degree. And finally, I'm a writer myself, of both historical fiction and non-fiction books. So you can see that I'd be interested in the idea of writers creating and enhancing their own products.

During 2016 I was the Writer in Residence for the British Library's Business & IP Centre, in London, thanks to a generous grant from the Leverhulme Trust. Part of that time was spent working with writers across a series of workshops that became this book. I hope that my own experience, as well as the input of many working authors, will make this book one that you'll benefit from as an author.

And my own merchandise? It's in the pipeline and I'll talk you through it later on.

This book is written for fiction and non-fiction authors

alike. There's a list of resources at the end of the book, including titles that I have found useful and which I hope you will too.

Throughout this book you'll find little sections called 'Top Tips', and 'Exercise'. These are designed to get you to use this book interactively and get one step closer to having your own merchandise and products by setting your mental gears in motion.

Top Tip

A *book* can, of course, also be merchandise; think colouring books, books that act as a 'workshop' style journal companion to work through a non-fiction book and so on. A non-fiction book might come out of a fiction book as a piece of merchandise, and vice versa. For example, you might write a children's story about dealing with feeling angry as a piece of merchandise if you've written a non-fiction book on how to deal with toddlers (their behaviour, problems, etc.). Or you might have written storybooks about how children can deal with their feelings and then team up with a professional in that field to write a non-fiction book for parents on how to help children deal with their emotions.

2. Why develop author merchandise?

Have you ever visited Shakespeare's Globe theatre? If you have, cast your mind back to the gift shop. If you haven't, then a quick view online will show you the contents. There must be hundreds of products: badges, Globe Experience vouchers, jewellery, snow globes. Visit Etsy online (www.etsy.com). Put in 'literary' as your search term and watch as hundreds of products appear: *Pride and Prejudice* confetti, poster prints of quotes from *Jane Eyre*, and *Alice in Wonderland* shoes. Literary merchandise is big business. Of course, the works I've mentioned so far have some advantages: they are major classics that everyone knows and loves. Also, their authors are dead and their copyright has expired, so anyone is free to make money from them. But consider that indie bands and film-makers also create merchandise. Why shouldn't authors do the same?

Merchandise is a valuable part of creating your 'platform' (also known as 'visibility') as an author. If you haven't yet read Chuck Sambuchino's book, *Create Your Writer Platform* (Sambuchino, 2012), then please read it as soon as possible. It's a great read and the only book I've ever read that really explains platform for writers properly and gives practical ideas for creating it, both for fiction and non-fiction writers. He says that 'platform, simply put, is your visibility as an author'. Platform is your website, your network, your authority and credibility; your committed fans ready to buy your books; your outlets and so on. Merchandise has a part to play in developing your platform and it will become a more visible and important part of many writers' portfolios as time goes on.

Merchandising only used to be for the superstars of the writing world – Stephen King, Terry Pratchett – not for the lowly author making an ordinary living at their writing, or even writing part-time. Creating products and distributing them was expensive and so a lot of merchandise was only created for books that made it as film productions, or for famous, long-dead authors. Merchandising was out of anyone else's league.

But the costs have come down and people's creativity has gone into overdrive. It has also become harder to reach readers because there are so many different outlets for media of all forms. So the more channels of communication you open, the better your chance of finding your audience. There is also evidence to say that hearing about content or authors from several different sources encourages people to pay more attention. Now writers are beginning to consider merchandising and are creating their own exciting products. These enhance the writer's visibility, thus improving and developing their platform, and also have the capacity to bring in income – always a good thing in a profession that is notorious for paying badly! Products can add to your readers' experience of your writing or help other writers develop their craft; they can bring new readers to you; and give you authority on a given subject.

Having your own merchandise is now an option for every writer.

Ready to get started?

Exercise

If you'd like to see some serious quantities of literary merchandise in action, visit the gift shops of the following places, in person or online:

- The British Library (www.shop.bl.uk)

- Etsy (www.etsy.com)

- Shakespeare's Globe theatre (www.shakespearesglobe. com/shop)

- Zazzle (www.zazzle.co.uk): check out Stephen King's page, whose merchandise profits go to The Haven Foundation, an interesting choice by an author who presumably makes enough money from direct book sales to be able to turn his merchandise income to more charitable uses.

You'll get many ideas and realise just how important merchandise is to an author's visibility.

Top Tip

You can, of course, also develop merchandise from out-of-copyright books that are relevant to your own work. For example if you are a historical-romance writer you could have a set of merchandise featuring great romantic heroes or heroines, from Mr Darcy to Heathcliff, Jane Eyre to Emma, because it will draw the kind of person that might want to read your books. If you write about vampires, then *Dracula* merchandise would fit you better. As a general rule of thumb a book will go out of copyright seventy years after the author's death, but you *must* check each item individually. Contact the British Library's Business & IP Centre for help with this (see Resources). Check illustrations separately because the illustrator for the same book will almost certainly have died at a different time!

3. Products vs. merchandise

It is important to clarify the difference between 'merchandise' and 'product'. I am aware that most people – me included – often use them interchangeably. But there is a difference, which is worth being aware of when you're developing your own.

Of course most merchandise *is* a product, but a product is not always merchandise, and you need to think about this when developing your own products. *The Oxford English Dictionary* says that merchandise can be defined as: 'products used to promote a film, pop group, etc., or linked to a fictional character'.

This is worth focusing on. By merchandising I mean a product that is heavily linked to something in your writing. If JK Rowling develops a wand product that is 'merchandise', because the product is directly linked to the *Harry Potter* books and the reader's experience of them. Once you have read those books then a wand ranks pretty highly as something you'd like to have (maybe just secretly, if you're a grown-up!). If, on the other hand, JK Rowling developed a range of notepads, then clearly there would be a link to her as a successful writer, but not really to the *Harry Potter* books and the reader's experience of them. So that, to me, would simply be a 'product'.

Clearly your product should not undermine you or your writing in any way, but one is not necessarily better than the other and you could certainly develop a product that does not link to your writing. However, be aware of the difference. So now, when I use these terms, you'll know what I mean.

Exercise

If you are published in the traditional way, check your contract to see if you still retain the merchandising rights to your books. Chances are that you do, as they are often excluded from other rights sold to publishers, which means you are free to develop your own products and sell them. If the merchandising rights have been sold but the publisher has done nothing with them, then find out if you can get them back. The publisher might welcome this, as you would be enhancing the product in which they have invested.

If you are a self published author (what I would refer to as an 'indie' author) then obviously you don't need to check your contract and you can develop whatever you like.

4. Five things merchandise should do for you

Your merchandise/product is not just there to look pretty and make you feel like a 'real' writer. It needs to work for its living, like the rest of us. There are five things that your merchandise or products should be able to do for you. It's unlikely that every item will tick all five boxes, but it should achieve at least one of these things; the more the better. Think carefully about this when choosing which products to develop. If an item ticks all five boxes then I think you're looking at a top-notch piece of merchandising or product. If it doesn't do at least one of these things, then you shouldn't bother with it.

1. Bring in income

Writing isn't known for paying a lot unless you hit the big time, so all income streams should be gratefully accepted, and I would advise most writers to try and develop a portfolio of sources of income. One of these can most certainly be products and merchandise. Think how much money the *Twilight* range of merchandise must bring in. Remember, though, that your chosen products need to be profitable, so that if they sell well, you'll actually make money on them.

Top Tip

Make sure you are very clear on how much each product costs to make and sell – don't forget about postage and your time input, for example – and how much profit will be left over. Also, if it will be made up-front, rather than made to order, think about where it will be stored and whether this will have cost implications. Don't make a product that doesn't make at least a small net profit, otherwise you are just giving gifts away.

2. Add to your credibility

Take a look at the case study of Randy Ingermanson (the Snowflake Guy, p.50). As he teaches writing, a piece of writing software naturally gives him additional credibility; it gives him something unique to bring along to his teaching, as well as a product to sell to his students. This is also true of Shaun Levin's Writing Maps (p.52); it gives him something fun and different to offer his writing students.

Exercise

Is there another part of your writing portfolio you could support with a product? Do you teach creative writing or some specific aspect of it? Do you offer public speaking? Do you teach literacy, or work with people to develop their creativity? Many writers work in multiple other roles related to their work, such as teaching writing in prisons or schools, authoring textbooks, developing websites for other creative people, and so on. Is there a product you can develop to add credibility and fun to your other roles as a writer?

3. Increase your readership

If a product you've created sparks someone's interest, chances are it will also spark their interest in you and your writing – even if it's not merchandise. They may seek you out even if they were not a reader of yours before, and if they enjoy your work, then you have just signed up a new reader. There are genres I'm not that keen on reading as a general rule, but if I see some really fascinating merchandise linked to a book in that genre I might give that book a try because it has captured my attention and drawn me in, and I already like something about it: perhaps a quote or an image. I might even like the merchandise and buy the book for a friend who I know enjoys that genre... and *they* might become your new reader.

Top Tip

Many writers offer a free sample of their writing – a short story, novella or even full-length book – as a means of building up an email-marketing list. If you do this, then it's a good idea to have your free book link available wherever your products are on sale – even on their packaging – so that a non-reader can easily try out your writing. Having a free book to draw in new readers is a common marketing strategy amongst many writers, as it lowers the perceived risk of trying you out for the first time. Remember that you are a writer first and foremost, so the products and merchandise should always lead back to you. Someone may love your products first before they love your books, so give them an easy way to become a fan of your books as well.

4. Increase your visibility

Maybe the product sparks some interest but the person does not come to you straight away as a new reader. That's okay. They may enjoy your product anyway and your name will become known by more people. If a person is aware of you in a positive way they may mention you to others, thus improving your visibility. And who knows? *Their* friends and colleagues may become your readers. Visibility is platform.

Products also give you something interesting and different to share via social and traditional media, again giving you visibility, and people who buy your products will probably be happy to be on your mailing list, adding to your ability to reach out to a wider audience.

Top Tip

If you have a mailing list of people who have bought your products and you email them with a reminder to buy a new product, or at gifting times of year (Mother's and Father's Day, Valentine's Day, Christmas or other religious holidays requiring gift-giving, back to school gifts for children or end of school year gifts for teachers, etc.), then remember to mention your books as well – possibly as a gift for someone else. Someone might love your jewellery merchandise without liking your historical fiction, but they may have a parent, sibling or child who enjoys your genre. The same goes the other way round: let your faithful readers know that you have merchandise available when you contact them.

5. Enhance the reader experience

If you love a writer and their books then you want more of their writing; you want to spend time in their world. Take a look at Haruki Murakami's Diary app case study (p. 77) to see an example of this being done well. If you get that added experience, it should make you love their work even more and maintain your loyalty to them... and maybe bring along some fellow readers.

Many books are sold by word of mouth and merchandise

can enhance the desire to tell others about a beloved writer, especially if the items are visible, draw comment and questions (for instance, clothing, home-decor items and other products that are on or around a person). Clearly this is not going to be relevant where you are developing products that are not merchandise, but it is at the core of what merchandise is all about.

Exercise

Ask yourself: how can I share my world? What is your favourite location in your books? Is it based on a real place? What would evoke it for you: sounds, smells, images, textures, tastes? How could you recreate that for a reader who wanted to be part of your fictional world? Are there different seasons? Are there important names and locations? Is it a place they could actually visit? Would images of those places work well on merchandise? Can your readers eat or drink something from your world? Work your way through the senses and see what might recreate your world.

For non-fiction, you can still focus on the 'world' you are encouraging your reader to enter: the past for a history book; a relaxed world for a book on meditation; a world where the reader is a great parent/lover/ dancer/scientist, or whatever else your book is helping them to be. How can you make them feel that way?

5. Not just objects: Think laterally

It can be easy to stick with t-shirts and bookmarks, but do try and think more creatively about the possibilities. In particular, consider collaborating with another business for mutual benefit. This could open up a whole new range of ideas for you. Here are a few thoughts.

Affiliate marketing allows you to recommend products via your website: someone clicking on a link you have provided will earn you a little bit of commission. Websites with more links tend to get more visitors, so affiliate marketing can help you in more than one way. You can do this quite simply by joining affiliate programmes (like Amazon Associates (https://affiliate-program.amazon.com) and choosing ready-made products that are relevant to your books.

Take it a step further and try setting up affiliate links yourself with companies that might be right for you. As an example, you could contact a voucher experience company and ask that if you feature one of their products that is relevant to your books – e.g. your character loves to fly and they have a flying lesson available – would they: a) give you an affiliate commission; and b) a discount for your readers?

If you could get both of those, then your merchandise just became interesting: your readers got a connection to your writing; you got a really special piece of merchandise without lifting a finger; and you received a little bit of money as well. Meanwhile the company you're promoting acquired some extra marketing from an unexpected source. Everyone wins! Ask! You never know who will say yes.

Extra examples of how this might work:

A bespoke flooring company called Harvey Maria (www. harveymaria.com) (I'm sure there are others, I just mention these guys because I've used them myself). You send them a photo and they turn it into a piece of vinyl flooring. It's a lot of fun. So if you provide – on your website – a photo for which you hold the copyright and is relevant to your books, and which your fans could download and send to Harvey Maria, you would be turning *their* products into *your* merchandise.

Imagine if there was a picture on Terry Pratchett's website of the turtle holding up Discworld floating through space. If you were a fan, wouldn't you like that image on your floor? In that instance, you could either sell the high-resolution image – fans pay £5, for example, and you send them that image – or you make a deal with Harvey Maria as described above. Or both!

There's a company called Spoonflower (www.spoon-flower.com) that allows you to design your own fabric patterns. These are then available to order online and you get a 10% commission on each purchase of 'your' fabric. If you write about any kind of craft involving fabrics, this would be perfect for you. Equally, if you had some kind of design element in your fiction (e.g. your main detective owns a particular breed of adorable dog) then you could make up a print design involving that dog and make sure your readers know where they can order it.

If you believe that your target audience loves gardening and it's relevant to your book, then consider something like finding a rose with your favourite character's name. I tried looking for my own name – Melissa – which is not a very common name and found plenty of plants. Again, pair up with a gardening catalogue or company that might make a deal with you.

Think about 'services' as well as products. If you write about photography and how to take great pictures, would your most avid readers enjoy attending a photography workshop run by you? If you write about ghosts and live somewhere suitable spooky, what would your fans pay to join you on a walking tour a few times a year round your favourite *haunts*? (Sorry!) Plenty of non-fiction authors are now turning their books into online courses, but there could be opportunities for fiction authors as well.

Top Tip

It's not forever. Merchandise does not have to be a 'forever commitment'. If you're new to it, try something small for a specific promotion – perhaps a competition, a festival or the launch of a new book. With the advent of print on demand, there's no reason to spend a fortune on a pile of stock that ends up not selling. See how it goes. If it's a success, keep it as an ongoing item and consider whether it would be worth buying in bulk to lower your production costs. If you think it doesn't really work, then move on. This approach also works for collaborations: don't tie yourself in knots swearing undying love for one another, just agree to try something out together for a limited time and review progress. You might notice, in the food and drink world especially, that many organisations bring out a 'limited edition' or 'seasonal special' product. If it only does okay, they'll probably drop it and try something else next time. If it's a huge success, guess what? It will become a permanent part of their product range. This could be worth copying as an approach. Announcing an item as a limited edition also makes it sound more special!

6. Case studies: Regular writers

It's always useful to see some real, up-close case studies when you're trying to develop your own ideas. So I've chosen this first round of case studies because they feature 'ordinary' writers: ones you might not even have heard of but who are making a decent living by their writing without being multimillionaires. A few still have a day job to help pay the bills. So I hope you'll find these case studies accessible. You don't need millions to develop these ideas, you just need a good imagination – and most writers should be fine on that front. These writers were nice enough to answer a few questions for you!

Daniel M. Davis

Daniel is a graphic artist/illustrator and the author of several books, including *Caught Creatures,* a monster-haiku book, and a webcomic, *Monster Commute.* He works with his wife Dawna and has a large and varied merchandise range on his site Steam Crow (see link below). Below are some of his thoughts on the merchandise they've developed over time.

What kind of writing do you do?

I'm primarily an illustrator, though I do find writing to be an important part of what I do. I've written and illustrated five books (with my wife Dawna), from Monster Haikus to alphabet books about what monsters do when Hallowe'en is over. Of late, I've been writing fiction about the 'Monster Scouts'; a group from 1903 who 'Believe, Study, and Protect Our Monster Friends'. Somehow this became a real fan group, with Monster Scouts dressing up and meeting us at events and conventions.

What is your product/merchandise?

We make prints, buttons, resin-cast toys, hand-printed t-shirts, and Monster Scout gear, like Spirit Badges, bandanas, and anything else that we can find that is 'camp-' or 'Scout-related'. We've been finding vintage-style backpacks and screen-printing our art on them.

How do you choose what to make?

Basically our approach is simple: we need to be authentic and true to our interests, instead of simply chasing money. If we love something, there's a good chance that other folks will find it interesting too. Not everyone, but that's okay.

How do you get the products made?

We design most everything in-house, and then source companies to manufacture and/or print the things for us. Basically, since we're a micro-company, we try to find companies that already make what we need.

Any hiccups along the way?

Sure, that's part of how it goes. Sometimes things take five times longer to get in hand; other times, the quality is bad, or sometimes we simply make a mistake.

Best/worst things about it?

Best: Being your own boss, being the Creative Director so that we're proud of what we make, connecting directly with our audience and patrons.

Worst: Having to fund all this ourselves; doing bookkeeping and taxes; having to manage hundreds of different tasks and things; working constantly, with few days off a year.

What's the response from your readers?

Generally, it's been great. Sure, over the past decade there have been products that don't connect so well with folks, but the longer we do this, the more folks seem to understand and be excited about what we do. We certainly need to reach more people, but we're always working on that too.

What does merchandise do for you?

A combination of things: it's hard to say that just one is of primary importance. Income is vital; we make some money from our books, but the merchandise sells the best for us. BUT, if it doesn't connect with our core audience, it's not so helpful. The products themselves should help paint the story of what we're doing… seeing

37

a bunch of backpacks next to some badges and a huge banner that says 'Monster Scouts' – with pictures of monsters on them – all reinforce the message that we're trying to get across.

The products themselves need to enhance our audience's experiences, and having t-shirts and products in the world helps increase the overall brand visibility.

Do you have plans to keep having merchandise?

Well, you're speaking to someone who is primarily merchandise, so yeah, we're always inventing new stuff to sell. We use the merchandise to get people into our narrative, so we're doing it a little in reverse from how established writers might try it. Our strategy has been simple: you probably don't know us, but we'll use every way that we can to demonstrate to the world that we're building: be different, stand out, and have every product help emphasise this ecosystem.

www.steamcrow.com
www.monsterscouts.com
www.facebook.com/steamcrew

Exercise

Steam Crow almost work backwards, creating a wide range of merchandise which helps them to create a fantastical monster world, and fans who are then keen to buy their books. They are working within a community that likes to get together and display their preferences: think Comic Con and the huge numbers of attendees who dress up. What community does your work appeal to? Some societies that revere particular authors can have huge memberships and very loyal fans. Perhaps coming at it the other way round – products first – might create a world that you can then write about. What fascinates you? Is it miniature worlds, exploring nature, a particular kind of animal/fish/bird, creating extraordinary shapes with glass, or something else? What world could you create that people could visit through both products and books?

Lucy Furlong

Lucy Furlong is a writer and walking artist. Her poetry map, *Amniotic City*, was featured in The Guardian and her pamphlet, *clew,* was published by Hesterglock Press in 2015. Her latest poetry map, *Over the Fields*, was published in September last year. She is Writer in Residence at The Museum of Futures, Surbiton. She has set up a community writing group there which meets once a month, called Seething Writers. She is currently organising events and workshops for National Poetry Day and then will be planning the first Seething Writers publication.

How did you start making your merchandise and what is it?

I self-published my first poetry map, *Amniotic City* in October 2011, and at the time was very excited about the whole process of production and creating something different, and didn't really have any specific ideas about marketing or merchandising to go along with it, although a friend of mine did design a web site for me, and the maps were sold at readings, through a couple of bookshops and via Paypal on my web site.

Any mistakes early on?

I could have sold the first edition of *Amniotic City* much faster had I marketed it via social media and through some kind of merchandising gimmick. There was also a poetry reading where I lost five copies of the map, as people assumed they were free, possibly because of their pocket-sized format. To stop this from happening again I ordered some clear self-sealing bags, and price stickers, which meant people immediately realised they were for sale!

What does the merchandise do for you/your books/your readers?

Nearly a year ago, in September 2015, I self-published a second poetry map, *Over the Fields*, and had plenty of time and subsequent experience to feed into how I wanted to do it this time. Work-in-progress for the new map had already been exhibited as part of 'The Art of Walking' exhibition at Museum in the Park, Stroud, as part of the celebrations for Laurie Lee's centenery, and had a mention in the TLS.

Plus, in 2013 *Amniotic City* had been featured in The

Guardian, so my profile was raised somewhat and I knew I could do something special to launch *Over the Fields*.

So I printed a limited, numbered edition of 50 postcards, containing a brand new poem, which the first 50 people to buy the new map would receive, and this poem would only be available in this way. For me it was great fun to do, and I do think it helped to shift the first third of the limited first edition of 150 copies...two thirds of which have now gone in less than a year – whereas *Amniotic City* took years longer to sell. Each *Over the Fields* map is sent out in an envelope with beautiful photo stickers, specially made from photos taken of the place where the map is based, and each one comes with an *Over the Fields* postcard in full colour, which I write a message on. The limited edition poetry postcard is now sold out. I hope that this merchandise makes the product more enticing, satisfying and interesting, and that the limited edition postcard poem added something possibly different and hopefully of value.

What have you learnt along the way?

It is worth thinking about the added extras because for something like my map, which is more of an artefact, rather than a book, it is possible to be creative and playful with merchandise. It is also something that other poetry publishers and publications offer, as poetry seems to lend itself to this. I have learnt that it is good to create a niche for yourself and to make the effort to do something different as it appeals to collectors and piques people's curiosity.

Future plans for your merchandise?

I have recently revisited the area of the map of *Amniotic City*, five years on, to write new poems, which I read at the Walking Women event held at Somerset house this Summer. I hope there will be a second edition of *Amniotic City* at some point and that I can do something with this new poetry as a form of added extra / merchandising.

I have done one walk in situ for *Over the Fields* and hope to do more and I am sure this will lead to more merchandise being offered in relation to this in the future.

www.lucyfurlong.com
www.seethingography.wordpress.com

Exercise

Consider whether your merchandise can include a personal touch from you, the author, to your reader. Lucy's message written on the postcards adds something which her readers probably feel is very bespoke and unique to them and this will make them feel loyal to Lucy and her work.

Jonathan Green

Jonathan is a freelance writer of speculative fiction, with more than sixty books to his name. Well known for his contributions to the *Fighting Fantasy* range of adventure gamebooks, and numerous Black Library publications, he has also written fiction for such diverse properties as *Doctor Who, Star Wars: The Clone Wars, Sonic the Hedgehog, Judge Dredd* and *Teenage Mutant Ninja Turtles.*

He is the creator of the *Pax Britannia* series for Abaddon Books. The eighth novel set within this alternative steampunk universe, featuring the debonair dandy adventurer Ulysses Quicksilver, is *Time's Arrow* (2012). In 2015 he also put a dark, steampunk spin on a children's classic, when he published *Alice's Nightmare in Wonderland* (2015). As well as his fiction, he has also written a number of non-fiction books, including *Match Wits with the Kids* (2008), *Christmas Explained: Robins, Kings and Brussel Sprouts* (2014), and *You are the Hero: A History of Fighting Fantasy Gamebooks* (2014). He spends most of his time behind a keyboard in West London.

Jonathan is an expert on Kickstarter, having successfully raised funding for several books, including *Alice's Nightmare in Wonderland*, for which he decided to release a colouring book as a piece of merchandise to take advantage of the wonderfully gruesome illustrations his illustrator had come up with. The colouring book was so popular it went on to outsell the book and has won huge praise.

Why did you first develop merchandise?

I first developed merchandise to support a crowd-funded Kickstarter project, called *You are the Hero: A History of*

Fighting Fantasy Gamebooks. To produce a book, paying for artwork, as well as to print the thing, I needed to raise more than just the cover price of the book. The best way to do this was to offer items for sale to backers of the project that they would not be able to get anywhere else. Because *Fighting Fantasy* gamebooks used two dice, a pencil and an eraser, I offered a branded set of these to backers, along with things like art prints of the new artwork commissioned for the book.

Would you do it again?

Yes. In fact, I have done several times already. But I'm always honing what I do. I try to tailor the merchandise to the particular project, but I've also discovered that some things just don't seem to sell, like t-shirts. Well, not *Shakespeare vs. Cthulhu*-themed ones, anyway (2016). One of the most successful items I produced was a themed deck of playing cards for my *Alice's Nightmare in Wonderland* gamebook, which can be used to play the game, and which feature the artwork from the book on the picture cards.

What did you learn?

Loads! Not to over order stock, to begin with. Although it's nice to have something to sell at events, people generally just want to buy your books, so I restrict the merchandise to the specific crowd-funding projects, offering them as unique rewards to people who back the project, giving them the opportunity to own something that they wouldn't be able to otherwise. When it comes to crowd-funding, you have to make sure that you add the cost of producing the merchandise rewards – and any postage involved in having them shipped to you – to the overall target, otherwise you will be out of pocket at the end of the day, which is not the point of running a crowd-funding project!

What has been the customer response?

Generally, very good. The playing card thing is something I am going to do again for my next gamebook Kickstarter, *The Wicked Wizard of Oz* (due for publication in 2017). It becomes a talking point as well, and if you ensure that the merchandise is of a high quality, it helps enhance your reputation as well.

What do you feel merchandise does for you?

At the end of the day, it helps me raise enough money to keep producing the kind of books I want to write. However, it also fulfils a desire to create something cool/unusual/unique that wouldn't exist otherwise. And it certainly helps to enhance the appearance of my workspace.

www.jonathangreenauthor.blogspot.co.uk

Top Tip

Have a look through crowd-funding websites such as Kickstarter to see the kinds of 'rewards' offered to backers by authors such as Jonathan. Essentially,

> most of these are merchandise. They are generally products – with some experiences – that link to the idea that is being funded. From lunch with the creator to t-shirts or bespoke copies of a book, these websites can be a great source of ideas for your own merchandise endeavours.

LISA J HOBMAN

Bestselling author Lisa J Hobman writes romance with some mature content. Her debut novel, *Bridge over the Atlantic* (2013), was shortlisted in the Contemporary Romance category of The Romantic Novel Awards 2014. She now has nine romances available. She is a happily married mum of one, with two crazy dogs, and especially enjoys being creative. Her past jobs have included working as a singer and running a craft business, but writing is her full-time occupation.

In 2012 Lisa and her family relocated from England to their beloved Scotland; a place of happy holidays and memories for them. Making the move north of the border has given Lisa the opportunity to spread her wings and fulfil her dream. Writing is now a deep passion and she has enjoyed every minute of working towards being published.

As one of Lisa's main romantic heroes plays the guitar, she offers merchandise that declares the wearer to be one of his groupies – a neat twist on merchandise not being all about you but about your characters – thus engaging the reader with the world she has created.

Why did you decide to develop merchandise and how did you choose what to make?

Bridge over the Atlantic was my first foray into writing with a view to publishing, and so I was very new to the concept of publicity and how best to get my name out there. It was actually a reader who told me that the catchphrase of my main male protagonist would make a great t-shirt! The quote 'Don't bloody sing along' features in the book a few times. Greg is a pub musician, but he is quite a brusque character and not particularly a people person! When he performs at the local pub in the story he informs the audience that there is nothing worse, as a performer, than when the audience tries to join in and ruin a good song. He means it tongue-in-cheek… or does he?

So the idea for t-shirts and tote bags with the 'Don't sing along' slogan became something that my readers could own and that would remind them of my story. It also served as excellent merchandising as the title of the book and my author name were also visible on the items, and so anyone whose interest was piqued could look me up.

My mum is a very talented jewellery maker. It's been a hobby of hers for a few years now and she helped me to come up with ideas to produce themed jewellery items that would tie in with my stories. I have made earrings, necklaces and key chains with charms that link in simply. For example, the key rings that tied in with *Bridge over the Atlantic* would have a guitar charm, which linked the item to Greg; *Through the Glass* (2013) features Flick, an artist, and so the items for that book had a little silver artist's pallet on them. I also made items of merchandise that incorporated the book covers. However, due to copyright these items were only used for giveaways as I couldn't sell the image myself.

Has it done well for you? And if so, do you sell online or at events?

The merchandise that I have given away – most of it, to be honest – has been great in that it has created interest in my work for publicity purposes. I tend to give most of my merchandise away rather than sell it. If I have sold it at events it has been for a nominal fee to cover the cost of purchasing the elements included, such as charms and beads, bags and t-shirt transfers. I attend a few signing events a year and the merchandise is a great way of starting up conversations with potential readers. Many will enquire as to the significance of the charms I use, for example, and the slogan t-shirts are great fun!

Any lessons learnt?

I think the biggest learning curve is around what items people are interested in and what they don't really care for. I had some pens printed up with my author details and tag line on and they go down a treat! Great publicity, because who doesn't need a pen, and a good way of getting my name out there without massive expense. I have gone to the lengths of creating mugs and mouse mats in the past, but these were very expensive and not quite as successful for publicity reasons. Although many people presume authors make a tonne of money, we don't, so I am now having to curb my creativity and limit the amount of merchandise I use, in order to keep expenses to a minimum.

Any future plans in the pipeline?

I think I will continue to make jewellery that relates to my books and package the items in the way I have been doing; that is, in clear plastic bags which contain a card with my author logo and contact details. That way, the readers I encounter take away something pretty to wear/ use and they also have something they can refer to in order to look up my work. I won't be spending money on more expensive ways to create items and this is simply because I have had to change my mindset and really start to treat my writing as a business and not just a hobby!

www.lisajhobman.co.uk
www.5princebooks.com

Exercise

What would your characters create if they had their own merchandise? Are any of your characters rock stars, film-makers or stars, or even authors? Do they own their own companies or shops? Items that allow your readers to enter the world you have created for them can be a lot of fun, especially if they are amusing or thought-provoking.

RANDY INGERMANSON

Randy has a Ph.D. in theoretical physics. He's the award-winning author of several novels, has been teaching fiction for over a decade and is the author of *Writing Fiction for Dummies* (2009). He publishes the *Advanced Fiction Writing* E-zine, which has over 15,000 readers.

Randy's also known as 'the Snowflake Guy', because he developed the Snowflake Method of writing, which allows writers to plan their books from a one-line hook into a completed manuscript. The method is available for free online, which I admire about Randy: his website is full of free material that can help you to develop your writing. But he has also created a piece of software you can buy called Snowflake Pro, which helps writers by taking them step by step through the Snowflake Method and holding all their material ready to be brought together into the final product. He's used his own twenty years of experience in writing software to create a product that helps him write his own fiction, brings in income and affirms his reputation as a teacher of fiction writing and a speaker on the subject.

What made you develop the software?

The reason I developed my Snowflake Pro software was

so I could use it myself. I'd been using the Snowflake Method for years to develop my story ideas for my novels, but there were some repetitive tasks that I wanted to make the computer do so I wouldn't have to. And I figured that if the software was useful to me, it would be useful to other writers also, so I might as well earn some money by making a product and selling it.

What did you learn from the experience?

What I learnt is that it's not enough to have a good product. You also need a good marketing plan. Fortunately for me, the Snowflake Pro software is very well aligned with my website, since most people discover my website when Google leads them to my Snowflake article. This page has been visited more than five million times, and many of these visitors then move on to the sales page for Snowflake Pro. This means that marketing happens automatically. People who are interested in writing fiction come to my site, get excited about the Snowflake Method, read the sales copy about my software, and then buy it. It's all very natural and doesn't require a lot of marketing by me (which I don't like doing, because I hate to be pushy).

What's next?

I'd like to make a web-application version of Snowflake Pro. There are some advantages to a web-based version, but it's unclear whether this is what people want. But I'll experiment and see if people actually use it. I don't have a lot of other products in mind because my main focus needs to be on writing my own fiction, not teaching other people how to write fiction.

www.ingermanson.com
www.advancedfictionwriting.com

Exercise

What skills can you bring from your former and/or current jobs to create your merchandise? Randy knew how to develop software, so creating Snowflake Pro was something he could create himself rather than needing other people. I have a past history of working with food and drink products, so those are items that interest me most when it comes to merchandise, because I understand the pros and cons, as well as having some decent contacts in that industry. I also enjoy writing about historical food and drink in my novels, so people who enjoy them would be likely to appreciate food or drink merchandise. What skills and interests, contacts and knowledge do you have that could become good merchandise?

SHAUN LEVIN

Shaun developed Writing Maps: illustrated folded maps with creative-writing prompts, inspirational quotes and a recommended reading list. The Writing Maps are aimed at writers of all levels and interests, and they quickly grew into a wide-ranging series of almost twenty (so far), covering locations as diverse as the seaside and your own house. These are so popular that Shaun is now commissioned to create bespoke Writing Maps, both in the UK and abroad. The series also then spun off into creating a range of notebooks, which offer writing prompts for writers to explore certain topics such as food, family or cities. The products are stocked across the UK and USA, as well as on his website.

Shaun's own writing includes fiction and creative non-fiction. He's published a novella, *Seven Sweet Things* (2012), a collection of short stories, *A Year of two Summers* (2005), and several smaller works: *Snapshots of the Boy* (2009) and *Isaac Rosenberg's Journey to Arras* (2008). He's had short stories published in journals and collections alongside such writers as Ali Smith, Nadine Gordimer and Edmund White.

Shaun has taught writing for twenty years in colleges, schools, adult education and other settings, and run workshops in art galleries, bookshops, cafés, parks, a cemetery and a zoo. He is the founding editor of the literary journal *Chroma* and the director of Treehouse Press. He also writes the blog *20 Minutes on Writing*.

Shaun's Writing Maps and their spin-offs are not actually merchandise in the manner discussed at the start of this book. They are products, because they do not draw you into Shaun's own writing. However, they are a great example of a product that can create a whole new income stream that is relevant to your career as a writer and, in Shaun's case, also as a teacher of creative writing. A good tip to note is that Shaun keeps his products and his own website separate, as befits something which is a product rather than merchandise, although sensibly he does cross-reference them!

What gave you the idea for the Writing Maps?

After teaching for twenty years and also publishing for about twenty-five years, I thought it was time to put all of that experience into a book! I wanted to do something a bit different. I figured the world didn't need another creative-writing guide, so my challenge was to find a way to replicate the experience of being in a creative-writing workshop, where you're given a prompt and you just run with it. I've always loved maps, especially artists' maps, and writing in public spaces is a central part of my practice as a writer, as well as a teacher. All those elements came together organically at some point and the idea for Writing Maps came into being. All the prompts on the Maps are ones I've used in workshops or in my own writing practice.

How do you physically get them made?

I source my illustrators and designer through the free-lancer website People Per Hour (www.peopleperhour. com), and then I have the Writing Maps printed at various printers in the UK. Mostly, I fold and pack the Writing Maps myself.

Any hiccups along the way?

Not really. Sometimes illustrators don't quite get the

concept, so it takes longer to explain and more work is involved in the collaboration, but that's only happened a couple of times. What I have learnt about working with designers/illustrators is that illustration, layout and typography are very different things. Just because someone is a great illustrator doesn't mean that they're going to know much about design and layout. That has been a vital learning curve for me. Now when I choose an illustrator to collaborate with, I look out for all those elements by examining their past work.

What are the best and worst things about them?

The best thing is when people really get the maps and what they're trying to do. They may look playful and child-friendly, but they'll prompt you to write some serious stuff. The most challenging thing is the constant marketing and hustling you have to do to get the Writing Maps into shops, and to get reviewers to write about them. The satisfaction comes when a buyer in a shop really loves them and takes them on. Then you know they're going to sell. The other great thing is collaborating with different illustrators to create the Writing Maps themselves. I hand them the prompts and they run with an idea, then we work on it together so that it matches the vision I have for the Maps as an object that is fun, creative, surprising and inspiring: objects that you'd want to carry with you.

What has been the response from customers?

On the whole, people really like them. Having an online

shop and seeing how many repeat customers I get is a good feeling. I think people like the surprise elements of the writing prompts; that the Writing Maps set them off in directions they weren't expecting to go in their writing.

What's next?

There's always more Writing Maps to do. At the moment there are twenty-one maps, and I have three or four in the pipeline, as well as a book.

www.shaunlevin.com
www.writingmaps.com
www.20minutesonwriting.wordpress.com

Exercise

Is there something you'd like to develop which is not directly merchandise but taps into your love of writing? Perhaps it could become a new source of income, rather than a day job that is irrelevant to your writing work. Could you write bespoke books for people (their family histories, family recipe books, good wishes for a new baby or wedding, etc.?), make commissioned works of art around words for public spaces, or write for a range of inspirational wall stickers (decals)?

Kathryn J. Martin

Note: I'm grateful to both Kathryn J. Martin and Hope Clark who have allowed me to reprint this article after it first appeared in Hope Clark's highly recommended Funds for Writers *newsletter* (www.fundsforwriters. com).

Back when already an author of one book, many magazine articles and years of weekly columns in regional newspapers, Kathryn thought of herself only as speaker – humorist as Miz Maudie. and 'inspirationalist' as herself – until realising she was the only one in her writers group earning a living totally from writing. Encouraged by professionals such as 'Minnie Pearl' of Nashville's Grand Ole Opry, early on she resigned as a college professor to go full-time into speaking and writing but has loved writing since the age of two when she scribbled on the family history page of her mother's Bible, then caught the writing bug when first published at 15. Her two books are *Believe It or Not, Mama Likes the Nursing Home* (1996) and *Long Way from Lonely* (2013). This is her story of how she developed a piece of merchandise that has stood the test of time.

Knowin' When to Hold 'em

Now I'll be the first to admit I don't know a thing about poker. If Kenny Rogers hadn't sung 'The Gambler', I wouldn't even know about holdin' and foldin'. But one thing I do know, there's a time to submit my works and there's a time to 'hold' 'em. And I know that because I came close to lettin' go at the wrong time.

Twenty and excited about entering a radio station's poetry contest, I rushed through the rules, eager to start writing. All night I lost myself in the narrator, an elderly lady on her porch reliving memories. I chuckled watching the children grow from playing to courting on the porch, I cried seeing the now-empty porch, and rejoiced picturing future reunions on the porch. The next morning, ready to mail my entry, I read the rules again and froze. I'd overlooked 'Whether or not your poem wins, it will become the property of the radio station'.

Whoa! With little chance of winning, I could never submit my poem anywhere else or use it myself? Disappointed, I slipped it in a drawer where it stayed for 15 years until I resigned as college professor to enter full-time the field of writing and speaking.

For my first tour, I retyped the poem on a more modern typewriter and had 100 copies made on plain white paper. The first evening, in costume as a storyteller, I quoted a bit of the poem and following as myself, mentioned it would be available afterward. I'd laid out 25 copies with a sign, 'Poems: Donation of any size' and while greeting folks heard a yell, 'Go get more poems!' Already all 25 had sold! I hurriedly brought in 25 more only to hear in another few minutes, 'Go get the rest of the poems!' Except for two to use for copying along the way, all had sold. It was the same each place on the two-week tour.

Back home I chose a ream of quality buff-colored faux parchment paper and learnt if I'd wait a few days until the store used dark brown ink, the printing could be done commercially for less money. From then on, whether driving or being flown I've taken the poems, although by request I changed the sign to 'Donation of Any Size: Suggested minimum $1'. People give from $1 to $5 or more, often framing the poem or using it as a gift.

Folks want to take something home from an event but not everyone can buy our books or DVDs. Smaller printed or craft items make buying possible for those who can't and *lagniappe* for those who can. (*Lagniappe* [lan' yap], an oft-used term here in Southeastern Louisiana meaning 'a little something extra'.)

If I'd entered that early contest and won, I'd have received eight copies of a cheap magazine with few readers. BUT, by holdin', that simple poem has touched thousands of lives over years of speaking across the United States and Canada, providing extra income each place.

Glad I decided 'No' to 'sold' and 'Yes' to 'hold'!

www.mizmaudie.com

Exercise

Is there something you have written on which your readers place a high value? Perhaps a poem, as in Kathryn's case, or a short story? It could be a non-fiction piece as well: maybe a great checklist to use at home, or a recipe, even a particularly striking element of a memoir. If you speak a lot at events then something simple like this that people are interested in having as a memento of the event could be a great piece of merchandise. As Kathryn has discovered, because it is well-presented people even use her poem as a gift or a piece of inspirational home decor. Also, because it is inexpensive to produce and Kathryn gives guidance on how much to pay for it, it is always going to be profitable. Simple can be wonderful. You can even put up a sign suggesting people can only buy a certain number, which simultaneously makes people want to get their hands on one and also suggests they might like to buy *more* than one!

7. New product development: Steps 1–6

So now that you're all fired up with lots of ideas and can't wait to get your own merchandise developed, it's time to get on with the nitty-gritty of actually getting products made. The New Product Development process (NPD for short) generally breaks down into certain key steps you can use to successfully take a product from just an idea into reality. These steps are used by product developers everywhere. I've made these into a diagram you can handily refer back to as a memory jogger, and have also written more about each step so you can understand the detail required.

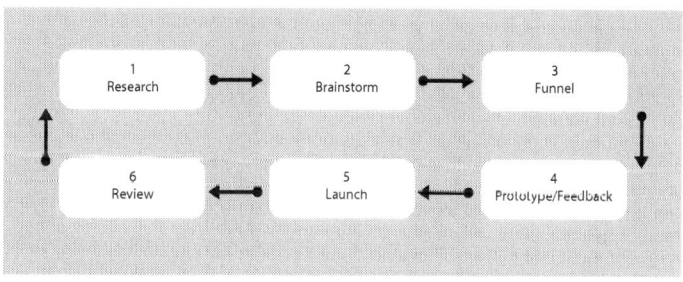

Figure 7.1. NPD Process, Steps 1–6

Step 1: Research

You need to know your market. This means two things: the people that you think are going to buy these products; and the competition. If your products are straight merchandise, then I hope that you already know who your readers are. And if not, then doing some research will be very illuminating for your general writing career. Who buys books in your genre? What do they do? What do they like? Where do they go? How do they dress, and so on? Ask yourself these questions and do some research.

Think about what other books your readers might like and have a look at who their target audience is, as there's likely to be a crossover. Once you have a good idea of who buys your books, ask yourself what other things they might like. Children like toys, sweets, adventure playgrounds, etc. Busy mums might like chocolate, home-decor ideas, jewellery and some peace and quiet (I know I do). Teenagers like music, films, clothes, their favourite singers, the latest social media, privacy, and so on. These are pretty generic ideas, but the more research you do, the more you will understand your target audience.

Now take a look at the competition. If you know of other successful authors in your area, do they have merchandise? What kind of merchandise is out there already that you think would appeal to your readers? Certain genres tend towards certain kinds of merchandise: sci-fi and fantasy have a lot of figurines and board games; kids' books have a lot of colouring and activity books, as well as toys. Don't just look at books, because in my opinion the book industry is a bit behind on the merchandise front, but also at films and music, because these areas have developed a lot of merchandise and may give you some good ideas. Look for the obvious (t-shirts) and the more unusual (jewellery).

Great places to check out are: gift shops in museums, art galleries and high-end or niche bookstores (such as Foyles' flagship, the National Theatre bookshop, the British Library shop). You can go in person or look online, because these are dedicated to products inspired by other items (often books or cultural artefacts). It's also worth looking through magazines or catalogues aimed at other markets, for inspiration on how to entice customers: from garden and kitchen catalogues to clothing and homeware brochures or websites. There are so many products you never knew you needed till you read about them!

Exercise

What would you want to buy? You probably enjoy reading books in your own genre, so what kind of merchandise attracts you, or would attract you? Many authors write for themselves first and foremost. I write historical fiction, which I love reading and so it makes sense for me to consult myself on what I'd like. For example, because I'm interested in food and drink *and* history, I have actually bought a bottle of mead (a medieval drink; alcohol made from honey), even though I don't drink alcohol, because that's how strong the curiosity level was for me when those two areas of interest came together. Also: I like history and I have children, so guess how quickly I bought them things like shields and swords, and so on, when we visited a castle gift shop? If I wrote for children, it would make sense to look at what products my own children enjoy playing with.

Step 2: Brainstorm

It's time to start throwing ideas around. You need a *lot* of ideas at this stage, so please don't hold back. Write down every possible idea for merchandise and products. It can be ridiculous; it can make you laugh out loud; it can be barely legal (please keep it this side of legal!); it can be offensive; it can cost a fortune; it can be barely linked to any writing at all. Just write it all down. Start by yourself, but this could also expand to a good exercise in a writing group; for example, take the writing of each person in the group one by one and brainstorm for it. Make sure to write down all the ideas. A big wall of post-its can be fun or just use a notepad.

To help you out, think about your books and what would match them well. Obvious links work well. Cooking books lend themselves to aprons and tea towels; horror books lend themselves to Hallowe'en masks; kids' books could link to a toy featured in the book. But think outside of that box too: perhaps a cooking book could be linked to a voucher experience to spend a day cooking.

Take a look at your own skills and contacts. Are you a software developer like the Snowflake Guy? Use that skill to create an app. Do you know someone that makes beautiful pottery? Then that's a contact you can draw on for advice and perhaps you could collaborate on something.

Think about your writing. Is there any merchandise hidden in there? If you read *The Hunger Games,* clearly a good item that leaps out at you is the Mockingjay brooch that Katniss wears. Is there a product within your pages already? Or a theme that would work well (flowers, locations, a character's collection of novelty teapots…)?

Please do include products that are not wholly within your control or seem too expensive or difficult to manage. For example, experience vouchers, airline tickets, garden furniture, and so on. Your task is to think of the ideal products, not the how, where and when.

A quick word on more general product ideas (i.e. not direct merchandise linked to your writing). If you're going down this path then, of course, you have a broader scope. However, I would just warn you of two things: one, make sure you still research your target audience; and two, don't undermine your own writing. If you are known for writing gentle warm-hearted romance where no one has sex before marriage and any bedroom scenes are rose-tinted, then developing a range of fetish gear on the side is not the way to go: it will undermine your writing brand.

Bonus! If you get stuck with too few product ideas and need a memory jog, then take a look at Chapter 16. You'll find a list of over sixty ideas, which you can read through to see if any of them might suit you. But do try on your own first as you might come up with something even better – and then write and tell me about it, so as this book gets updated I can feature you as a future case study!

Now that you have a tonne of ideas, gather them all up and put them away for at least a week. You can add to them if you suddenly think of something great, but it's important to take a break from this stage so that you come back to the ideas with a fresh pair of eyes.

Top Tip

If you already have avid readers, ask them what kinds of merchandise they'd like: they might come up with some good ideas! Ask if there is an object from your book that they'd like to have in real life. If you have lots of readers with whom you are connected, e.g. on social media, then a fun way to engage with them is to set up a survey or even a competition asking for ideas; the prize being either the merchandise itself or some other item from you (e.g. a signed book). Your readers love your books and they might pick out something you had never even thought of that they would really enjoy having. They will probably be flattered that you have asked and keen to be involved. If you announce the winners

and give credit to them for their ideas
then this will encourage them to spread
the word amongst their friends, which is
extra publicity for you.

Step 3: Funnel

So, that long list of product and merchandising ideas you made… you can't do all of them. Sorry.

It's time to get realistic now and that means you need to throw most of them out. You do this by *funnelling* your ideas. That means a lot of ideas go into the top of the funnel and only a few make it out the other side. Get out the list you made. Take a good look at it and cross out all the ideas you don't feel really excited about, because if you're not excited about them, you can't expect anyone else to be.

Now cross out the ones that, really and truly, you're not going to be able to produce right now, because you don't have the skills, connections or cash to make them a reality. For example, a product might be wonderful if made out of delicate china, as per your original idea, but rubbish If made in plastic, because that's all you can afford right now. I've seen this exact example at a major retailer who should have known better: it ended up in the Sale because no one would buy it. Don't sell an idea short, because if it's not made properly your intended customers won't like it either. Don't throw away these ideas, though. Keep them, because you never know when you might have what it takes to create them. But for now, they will not be included.

Now look at the list you have left. Hopefully it is much shorter. Highlight the ideas you really love and that other people have responded well to. Now think back to that market/customer analysis you did. Do you think your intended customers would like these products? Do they fit the market you've identified? Be a little harsh on yourself and the ideas: they need to *fit* the market, but not be clones. Don't be dull with your products, but don't be so weird that people will just be bemused.

I think you'll now have a very short list. I'm hoping it's less than ten items. I'm impressed if it's less than five. Well done! You have some potential products! Think about how they might work in combination and how they might reinforce each other. Should you make them available sequentially, or as a group so people can mix and match from your list? Put the list aside for now and sleep on it.

Next we'll have a look at what needs to be done to make a real product. Funnelling your ideas is a crucial step towards a great product.

Top Tip

Use Chapter 4 (Five things merchandise should do for you) as part of your funnelling process. It can be a checklist. Give each item on your list a tick for every benefit it could achieve. Any products without any ticks at all need to be removed from the list. The more ticks an item receives the better, and if any ideas manage to get five ticks then I think you have just found your ideal product(s). Here are those points again:

• Bring in income (remember, think profitability)
• Add to your credibility
• Increase your readership
• Increase your visibility
• Enhance the reader experience (less relevant for products than merchandise, of course)

Step 4: Prototype and gather customer feedback

A prototype sounds kind of flashy but it isn't really. You are simply doing a test-run of the product. This may be getting a t-shirt printed in two colours so you can choose which one looks best before committing to a larger order, or trying the chocolate that will be made into heart-shaped moulds for you. A company might do a mock-up for you to tempt you to place a larger order. You need to try and see how the real product will look/taste/smell/feel or even sound. Sometimes you'll get the exact product; sometimes it's a mock-up. The closer to the final item it is, the better.

Take a good look at it and ask yourself some questions.

Does it look the way you thought it would? Does it do what it's supposed to do? Does it taste how it was supposed to taste? And so on. If you have doubts about any aspect, then stop the process while you sort it out, otherwise you are just wasting your money.

Ask people for feedback and ask them to be as critical (constructively!) as possible. Strangers are better than friends for this exercise (don't ask your mother!). You could ask your readers via your website or take the product somewhere suitable: something for gardeners to a garden centre; kids' toys to a playground. People are often very interested in helping to develop a new product. If they ask to keep the prototype, you're looking at a promising item! Remember also to look at the packaging the item comes in – does it protect the product and show it off to best advantage? – as well as at the ordering process. Is it easy to order? How soon can the customer have it?

If you're going to handle the logistics, how storable is the product? Does it have a best-before date by which you will need to sell it? And how much room will it take up? Have you thought about things like padded envelopes and postage, and how many times a week you'll have to go to the post office? Or can you get someone to take over the process? This is where easy-to-use online sites such as Zazzle (www.zazzle.co.uk) or Café Press (www.cafepress. com) come into their own as you won't be dealing with the logistics: you simply design the products, set them up in a themed store and take a royalty when people order them.

Top Tip

Standing the test of time is really important. Make sure your product is good quality. A shoddy item will reflect poorly on your brand. If a t-shirt looks great but washes badly or fades quickly, the person who bought it will associate that failure with you. Choose good suppliers and check that the product behaves as it should. Make any particular ways of using/treating the product clear to users (e.g. washing instructions, or not leaving it outdoors). Be completely happy with it before you press 'go'. People are more willing to order the more comprehensive the guarantee. What will you offer for yours?

Step 5: Finalise and launch

Make any minor changes needed after having seen your prototype, finalise logistics and marketing materials (if needed). Press 'go'! Once the product is ready, do a couple of test-runs by buying it if the logistics are not in your own hands. If they are, perhaps do a 'soft' launch, where the products are available to a small or friendly audience, or at a minor event. This is common to make sure everything goes smoothly and to iron out any glitches. Once you've got past this phase, consider your products well and truly launched, perhaps at a big event or with a marketing push via social media, or linked to the publication of one of your books.

Top Tip

Don't forget about your merchandise! As with all products, it will not sell itself. If you have a website, use social-media platforms and/or send out regular newsletters or similar to your fans, make sure your products feature on *all* of those communication outlets. You don't need to sell, sell, sell if it makes you uncomfortable, but you can make sure your products are visible and not hard to find or buy. Perhaps have some fun with a specific item: use it as a giveaway in a competition; wear it in your profile photo; ask fans to send in pictures of themselves with it; or even take an item on your travels (a doll/soft toy/sculpture) and photograph it in funny locations; or get your readers to do this as a competition. Prizes can be more merchandise or signed books. Have it around your own home/ person/workplace etc. so that people can see it and comment on it. Perhaps give away a few items to people who might help to promote it, and so on.

Step 6: Review

Just when you thought it was all over... it very much isn't! From the moment your product becomes a reality, you need to review its performance. Are you happy with how it looks, who makes it, and the logistics? What have you learnt that you will apply to the next product? Has it provided you with any ideas for another product?

Keep an eye on progress. Does the product need to be updated? Does it look dated? What are your competitors doing? Is it a huge success, and should you hurry up and make it in more colours, more options to suit budgets, handbag sizes, and individual styles? Is it profitable or are the costs beginning to creep up? Conversely, is there an opportunity to have it made more cheaply while still sticking to your specifications?

When you have a range of products – for instance, Shaun Levin's Writing Maps – then consider the range as a whole. Is one item more popular than the others? Try and work out why and replicate that into the rest of the range, perhaps by tweaking it in some small way. Will the same concept work in a different format: tea towel into coffee cup; notepad into journal? Is it time to branch out into a similar or different product range?

If you've chosen to create products in collaboration, how is that relationship holding up? Is it time to work with someone else, or would you like to develop that relationship further?

Top Tip

Stick with the basic new product development (NPD) steps time after time. Remember: when you get all excited about developing a wider product range, take the time to go back through the Six Steps of NPD so that you don't miss thinking carefully through *all* the steps necessary to making a successful product. Every product developer in the world makes better products when they take it one step at a time.

8. More case studies: The superstars

The central premise of this book is that you *don't* have to be a bestselling author to develop your own merchandise. And with that in mind I've tried to use case studies of writers who are 'ordinary': making a normal-level living from their writing, or still working a day job. However, the 'superstars' of the writing world can be quite interesting as case studies, because what they choose as merchandise can give the rest of us some good ideas. So here are a few case studies where I think we can all learn something from the merchandise that's been developed.

Fifty Shades: From cheap to megabucks. Do what you can at the time

The merchandise of author EL James (Fi*fty Shades of Grey,* 2012) is interesting because you can see the transformation from not-that-well-known author's merchandise into mega-galactic-superstar's merchandise, topped off by a film series!

On EL James' website there are three initial pieces of content 'merchandise' which have then been developed onwards. The first is *On Location,* which is basically a gallery of pictures of places mentioned in the series (hotels, markets, bridges, etc.). It's simply a way of showing readers of the books what some of the places she describes actually look like. You could argue that the film series will take over this role.

The second is *Soundtracks;* a list of pieces of music that are mentioned in the books. There is now an actual CD that you can buy.

The third is wine lists. As the characters drink various wines throughout the books, EL James has listed them all here, together with the scenes in which they are drunk. The site also features two wines which have actually been named for the books (Red Satin and White Silk).

These three items are very interesting to me. Any writer, on a next-to-zero budget could have created the original items. They are not for sale, but they do add to the customer's experience of the books. Since the huge success of the books you can now see how each item has become tangible and monetised: a film (it could have been a calendar of the locations if you wanted a simple item of merchandise), a CD, drinks.

Exercise

It's worth thinking about whether you can create some zero-budget content merchandise for your website or blog, and how it might then develop. Perhaps you can find someone who might like to make one of those items a reality for a share of the profits. In the meantime, you will still be deepening your readers' experience of your world. If you already have these kinds of items on your site, then give some thought to how they could become a profitable product. And as for *Fifty Shades'* future merchandise... I don't think you've seen the half of what might be coming out soon!

Haruki Murakami's Diary app: Calendars for new worlds

Welcome to Haruki Murakami's surreal world. This bestselling author has written novels, short stories and non-fiction, but now there's an app that will take you right inside his world. Essentially it's a calendar app (*Murakami Diary*), but it includes quotes from his back catalogue, as well as six new and exclusive stories. The seasons are marked by cherry blossom and Japanese maple leaves, while cats (who turn up a lot in his books) slink through the pages. If you're a fan of his work, having the diary would be a lot of fun and a respite from whatever the day is throwing at you, although one hopes you wouldn't end up being late for your meetings because you are too wrapped up in reading just *one* more story.

This particular product is a very good example of merchandise because it constantly takes you back to Murakami's writing: reminding you of his books that you've enjoyed; making you curious about those you haven't yet read; enhancing your appreciation of his writing; and even giving you more of it on an exclusive basis. At the same time, it's not the most complex item. Basically, it's a calendar app to which has been added some nice graphics and content appropriate to the author.

So it's a simple idea, but one which works very well for those writers who have an unusual world available. It could also work well for historical fiction, as well as sci-fi, fantasy and non-fiction (e.g. an inspirational calendar to motivate you to achieve something).

Exercise

Can you think of locations that stand out for the reader in your books? What about celebrations from your period of history that the average reader might not know about, and might like to read more about? If you write sci-fi, are there aspects of your world you could expand on: key roles; the shape of your solar system; different planets; hierarchies and clothing?

For the non-fiction writers, consider links to your own story and what you were doing when you wrote the book (many people are interested in the locations where creativity took place), as well as which aspects of your work your reader could consider in more depth over time: could they have new habits to develop each month, or inspirational sayings on a daily basis? Could they have snippets of information to mull over, or new information to learn? New skills to practice and the space to do so (e.g. draw a picture every week) could work. Think of 365 days, 52 weeks, 12 months, 4 seasons...

Game of Thrones: Monopoly works for everything.

Monopoly has clearly worked out that its property-acquisition game can actually be tied into quite a wide range of successful media. Their version of *Game of Thrones* (Martin, 1996), for example, can't have required very much tweaking of the original layout. Board games are actually pretty flexible in this regard, and you could take a look at your own book and consider whether a board game would make good merchandise for you. You may think that only fighting/acquisition-type stories would work, but actually you only have to think of PG Wodehouse's comic creations of Jeeves and Wooster to realise that it would be quite easy to make that into a board game: travelling from aunt to aunt; being arrested for acquiring cow creamers; and getting mistakenly engaged to unsuitable girls; only to be saved by Jeeves in the nick of time.

Exercise

What was your favourite board game as a child? Do you have a game you play now, like *Candy Crush*? Have a look at retailers online to see what kinds of board games exist, and try a few out if they sound interesting. Experiment with a few ideas to see if your book/s lend themselves to a board game. You can buy dice, blank playing cards and other bits and pieces online, and use them to test out your concepts. A simple wipe-clean whiteboard and some markers will allow you to try out a board design several times, and adjust it until you're happy. When you're getting close to a good design, get the Industry Information Guide on board games to find out how to protect your inventions – and not infringe anyone else's copyright – from the British Library's Business & IP Centre. You can also consider apps of course, depending on what kind of budget, skills or contacts you have.

JK Rowling: Collaborations with food companies

From the vast array of merchandise available to choose from in the *Harry Potter* world, I'm going to focus on the food and drink. This is: 1) because Rowling has the most wonderful food and drink ideas; and 2) because I think that food is one of the easier merchandise ideas to work with, if you're willing to partner up.

The *Harry Potter* books have some amazing food and drink ideas: the *Every*-Flavour jelly beans, involving some nasty surprises; the Butterbeer; the Chocolate Frogs, which have collecting cards inside, and the frogs jump away and escape if you don't eat them quickly... These are some fantastic edible ideas unequalled except in Roald Dahl's *Charlie and the Chocolate Factory* (1964) – lickable wallpaper; and chewing gum that tastes like a three-course meal. Even if the *Harry Potter* books had never taken off to the extent they have, if they had remained far lower-key in sales but still much-loved by their readers, I'd argue that JK Rowling could easily have found a jelly-bean maker to make a few packets with some nasty twists inside: a great piece of merchandise for the books and a nice novelty product for a sweet maker.

Plenty of food manufacturers, especially smaller entrepreneurs, would probably be interested in teaming up with an author who had some fun ideas to turn into merchandise. If your books include special foodie moments for adults or children, then consider food or drink for your merchandise and hunt out some partners. The good thing about this is that you can also just team up on a temporary basis, not for life: a Christmas or Valentine's Day promotion, or a summer holidays/back-to-school push could be fun and a good way to try out a partnership if you're not quite sure.

Exercise

What kinds of food and drink appear in your books? Are any of them key to the plot? Would any of them help to recreate the feeling of your books for your readers, immersing them in your world? Do you know any food companies? Keep a look out in the news media for small food and drink entrepreneurs as they are most likely to be inventive and up for a possible collaboration. What you need is someone who makes something quite similar to what you have in mind, and who can easily alter a recipe or label to suit your needs without incurring huge start-up costs. Do remember that food and drink items, unlike many other products, are subject to use-by dates, so this is something to bear in mind when doing your planning.

A Clockwork Orange masterclass: Sharing the 'making of' a novel

There's an app for *A Clockwork Orange* (Burgess, 1962) that is essentially the 'making of' the novel, celebrating fifty years since it was first published. When you read the description it sounds closer to a 'masterclass' on the topic than a simple app.

It contains images of the original manuscript, which has illustrations and musical scores; insightful essays and introductions from a wide range of critics; and the audiobook version and audio discussions of themes from the book. It also contains videos of discussion groups, clips of the author reading from and discussing the book, a prologue and epilogue, interviews and articles.

I think if you work your way through the whole thing you probably deserve an honorary degree on the subject. Obviously this works well because it is a classic text, but it could act as a very nice item of merchandise if your book is unusual in some way – perhaps a comic book – and if you can put together some good material to accompany it: photos of real locations; preliminary sketches; short stories covering how certain characters came to join the story; a pre-mythology, etc.

Exercise

Consider whether you could put together enough interesting materials to grab your readers' attention. Can you write exclusive short stories, prequels or sequels? Offer videos of a book club discussing your book with you, and so on? Do you have photos of your own from visiting a location for research? If you give this piece of merchandise away for free as a way of collecting your readers' email address, it could work very well as a way of building up a marketing mailing list, which is worth a lot in future sales. Write down a quick list of things that might go into such a package and how easily you could provide them.

Quentin Blake: A lesson for author-illustrators

There are some writers who possess an additional skill beyond their writing abilities: for example, those people who are also the illustrators of their own work – usually, but not always, children's books or comics. This skill immediately offers the author a product that may or may not be merchandise, according to their choice.

The wonderful children's illustrator Quentin Blake has a website which includes a shop of merchandise: mugs, lampshades and greeting cards. Working in collaboration he has also created things like fabric and wallpaper using his designs. But on a very simple level, he also offers prints of his work, for approximately £100–£200, and this is something that any illustrator could offer. Bear in mind these are prints, not originals – an original Quentin Blake will set you back a lot more! – but you can consider whether you want to offer originals, prints, or even bespoke works like painting murals in people's houses based on your style.

Many people spend quite a bit of money on their baby's nursery, for example, and would probably be thrilled to have an original piece of art on the wall. When I decorated my kids' nursery I chose to use prints by some of my favourite children's illustrators, including Blake, and it was quite funny to watch my children realise, over time, that some of the pictures on the walls matched the pictures in their books.

You could also arrange for your designs to feature on wallpaper and fabric via Spoonflower (www.spoonflower. com) and on a wide range of other items at Zazzle (www. zazzle.co.uk). Consider what kinds of products your artwork would suit best, and go wild. Some drawings might be linked directly to a book (perhaps more details of the world you have created); some might simply stand alone as pleasing images in your style. I do think that any author-illustrator should most definitely consider using their talents to create a product range, whether selling prints, original drawings/paintings, taking commissions or, of course, putting some of their images onto other products.

If you are an artist as well as a writer, your merchandise range is ready-made. You only need to look at the vast array of products featuring an *Alice in Wonderland*

(Carroll, 1865) theme, for example, to realise what a gift being an illustrator is when it comes to merchandise. If you don't draw, but enjoy a graphical look, you could consider using some of your words as graphical elements on products such as a poster, on mugs, etc.

Exercise

One way to get your work more widely known could be to team up with design and fashion students at a university, or designer-makers on platforms such as Etsy (www.etsy.com). Find ways to collaborate, by which they can use your images on their products. You might share profits or you could simply use their work as a means of promoting your work, such as if a fashion student used your book concept as the theme of their graduating collection. Go to graduate end-of-year shows to get inspiration.

Julia Cameron: Turning books into other forms of media

Julia Cameron wrote *The Artist's Way* (1992), a hugely successful book for artists (especially writers), and one which produced some extra products to go with it, such as an activity book where you can jot down your replies to the writing tasks she sets you. This in itself could be a piece of merchandise; plenty of successful non-fiction books result in another book, which acts as a companion piece.

But the other direction non-fiction books can go in is

turning into an online course. This is because many people are more visual and prefer to follow things like videos. They also like to have more direct access to the author and feel that they are being guided through the material on a more personal basis than just reading the book. *The Artist's Way* is available as a book, for approximately £11, or as an online video course for £149 (www.juliacameronlive.com/the-artists-way). The course is a series of videos, which guide you through the book's material. The idea is that you should feel as though you are actually spending time with Julia Cameron; as though you are attending a creative-writing class with her. You may think that it's a lot to pay to access the same material, but as I said, some people prefer to access the material in a different way and are willing to pay for it, as it compares favourably to evening classes in terms of cost. Also, some online courses offer special bonus material or, for example, access to the author (perhaps a live Skype session or access by email or phone).

Exercise

If you've written a non-fiction book, then consider whether someone would like to access an online course covering the material.

If you have a recipe book you could demonstrate cooking some of the recipes. Perhaps you have a self-help book and people would like further details and exercises to work through. Perhaps you have a children's book that you illustrated, so you could have an online drawing class showing your readers how to draw their favourite characters. If you draw monsters, can you make a book for kids teaching them to draw monsters? If you draw animals or people, could you create an online video to teach people to draw the way you do? Many people would love to have a drawing class with an illustrator they admire. There are various online course platforms, such as Thinkific (www.thinkific.com), where you can develop your own course that is hosted by them. Look up something like 'platforms for courses' on Google, and check out different ones to see what suits you. Remember that people will be willing to pay much more than for a book, but that you must provide a quality product that adds value to the reader.

9. *Terrible* products: Don't go there!

This book wouldn't be complete without a warning. There are some examples of spectacularly bad merchandise out there. Google 'awful literary merchandise' or similar key words and enjoy the giggles that follow. If you develop anything dreadful there will be plenty of people amusing themselves at your expense for years to come. Don't undermine your brand by making something shoddy, tacky, offensive or deeply inappropriate. The worst two I've seen so far are:

1. A pair of oven gloves with 'Sylvia Plath' written on them – a poet who committed suicide by gassing herself with an oven. Please don't.

2. A sparkly dildo that can be put in the fridge to make it cold. This already pretty odd product was made worse by the fact that it was supposed to tie into the *Twilight* range, hence the sparkle and coldness. Not only does it sound like quite an unpleasant experience, but bear in mind that the series was initially supposed to be for young adults, which could well include underage children, as YA fiction is aimed at the 12+ market. Not suitable at all.

On the whole you ought to realise a product is not a good idea if it is:

- Inappropriate for the target readers' age.

- Refers to something inappropriate to make money from, such as suicide, murder, incest etc.

- Is poorly made so that it undermines your brand.

- Has no logical link to your brand at all: if your books are all-out action then let's face it, a perfume range is not going to be suitable. Jackie Chan has a skincare range, which makes no sense to me. However great you think either he or the products are, they just don't go together. If you write serious sci-fi then I'm not sure tea towels are the way to go... unless your starship's crew is badly in need of clean coffee mugs.

Top Tip

Good merchandise should reflect your value structure. So if you are writing about empathy with nature, your products should stress their ethical production. If you write about holding certain key values, perhaps your merchandise could give a percentage of profits to suitable charities. People buying merchandise are buying into your view of the world, and this can win friends if you describe something with which they agree.

10. Planning ahead and taking baby steps

In his very useful guide, *Sell Your Book like Wildfire* (2012), marketing expert Rob Eager talks about the irresistible lure of a list to help your sales. Referring primarily to non-fiction books, he suggests that you deliberately include what he calls 'book-marketing tools' when writing your book.

This could be a quiz (20 ways to know your relationship is in trouble), a list of questions (10 smart things to ask at an interview), secret codes to free web-based content, and so on. He found that by thinking ahead, when you mention a few extracts from such lists, perhaps at a book presentation, via social media or as a free handout, book sales increase markedly, as people's natural curiosity drives them to see the rest of the content to which you've referred.

Journalists also like lists as it gives them something to craft an article around. I can see how this works beautifully for a non-fiction book but I've actually also seen this done by a fiction author quite successfully. Bestseller *The Rosie Project* (2014), by Graeme Simsion, focuses on a man with Asperger's syndrome, who is trying to find a wife. He begins by using a questionnaire, which is, of course, horribly useless in actually finding him a soulmate. The full questionnaire is included at the back of the book, and it is quite funny to rate yourself against his (impossible) criteria. Or take a look at Matt Haig's lists in *Reasons to Stay Alive* (2015); life-enhancing and very quotable. Choose a good number: rounded numbers such as 5 or 10 items; or interesting numbers such as 7 or 13.

By the same token, merchandise opportunities can be embedded in your book by the simple strategy of thinking ahead. Rather than writing a book and then going back to see if there's any potential merchandise lurking in it and being disappointed, you can think ahead and place some opportunities within the book. Clearly, you don't want to crassly shoehorn these in so that they stick out like a sore thumb, but if there's something which fits naturally into your narrative, and you can gently enhance its presence by, perhaps, describing it in a little more detail, mentioning it more than once, or even increasing its importance within the narrative and plot, then do so.

A perfect example would be the Mockingjay brooch that Katniss is given and wears in *The Hunger Games* (Collins, 2008). Yes, the series is now a massive bestseller, but even if it hadn't been, that little pin – so carefully described, so easy to make in collaboration with a jeweller, so central to the storyline – is a wonderful example of the kind of think-ahead merchandise you could create. And it could so easily have been replaced with something far less simple to create.

Merchandise doesn't have to happen all at once. Let me tell you where I'm at right now: experimenting… or taking baby steps, if you like. One easy way to do merchandise is to take what's already out there and shape it to your needs. I write historical fiction set in the Forbidden City in China in the 1700s. It's a world of silk robes and concubines, exquisite surroundings and palanquins – that's a sedan chair to you and me, carried by bearers. I told you already I am interested, both by profession and personal greed, in food and drink. So one of the first pieces of merchandise I considered was flowering tea. These are unassuming little round balls, perhaps as big as a Ferrero Rocher chocolate, made of dried-up tea. Pour boiling water on them, though, and they miraculously unfurl to produce a flower in your teacup. They are *so* pretty, *so* Chinese and effortlessly give you a taste of my books. I started by using boxes of flowering teas as a gift for various people who had helped me with the book. They were thrilled and commented favourably on the link between the two, so I knew I was onto the right product.

How best to present them? I went online and amazingly found wedding favour boxes made in the shape of a traditional Chinese wedding palanquin, in red and gold, with tiny carrying handles. They just fit two balls of flowering tea. I can buy the boxes and the tea, even at a retail price, make them up and sell them for a nice profit while giving my readers a low-cost but charming way of entering the world I have created for them. They are perfect for events. I wouldn't much fancy offering them on my website, because I think they would travel badly, being very delicate. So I'll keep them just for gifts and events. Are the flowering teas in my books? Yes, because I deliberately placed them there, on the final draft of the first novel (planning ahead). The original text has a concubine, newly arrived in the Forbidden City, feeling overwhelmed by the luxury surrounding her, drinking a cup of tea with tiny flowers in it. I changed the text very slightly to describe a flower unfurling. It's not shoehorned in, you wouldn't even notice it... unless you had the flowering tea yourself.

What I'm investigating now, for a larger and more diverse range of merchandise, is Zazzle (www.zazzle.co.uk). They have a huge range of blank products onto which you can add your own designs and images. My favourites so far are little ceramic-tile coasters, lockets and cushions, but there seem to be literally hundreds of items available. You can then create your own 'store' – or multiple ones by theme or by book – and add your products to it. Zazzle will make the products to order, ship them and pay you a royalty that you have pre-set, making your life... well, pretty easy, I think.

Since I do research trips to historical locations and take lots of beautiful photos, this gives me some great images to work with. Meanwhile, you could also add text from your books to graphic wall posters, and inspirational quotes to coffee mugs. You can create a 'secret' store, while you design your products and get everything looking nice, and then unlock it when you are ready to reveal your creations to the world and start selling. Look out for my shop unlocking sometime in 2017 – and appearing on my website www.melissaaddey.com!

What else would work for my novels in the future? Perhaps voucher experiences featuring a maze, which is a romantic location in my first novel. Or flying Chinese lanterns, which appear in a dramatic night-time scene. There are a lot of possibilities once you start thinking.

Top Tip

People can get flustered by too much choice and end up buying nothing at all. This was tested in a well-known experiment on a random selection of food shoppers, when one jam stall had thirty kinds of jam available and the other had only six. Strangely, despite the limited choice, the stall with six jams sold to 30% of its visitors, while the stall with thirty kinds sold to only 3%.

Your customers may become frozen by too much choice, so even if you get really excited by developing your own merchandise, don't go overboard. Select your very best three to five items, for example, and stick to them. If you do end up eventually creating more than this, consider showing them in groups, e.g. clothing/food/experiences, or by the book/series, or in sets (e.g. a set of matching coasters or themed home decor), so that, again, the customer is only shown limited initial choices and then chooses again once inside the category. Less is often more.

11. Where to sell your merchandise

Obviously, on your website would be a good idea. There are simple plug-ins for most websites so that you can undertake transactions and, as I've already mentioned, you can have them set up somewhere like Zazzle (www.zazzle.co.uk) and simply provide a link on your site – with some enticing images of course! – to your 'store' there.

If it's an affiliate product/experience then just create a link to the site that is selling the product. One of the best places for selling merchandise, however, seems to be events, such as writing/book festivals. Having the merchandise right there in front of customers seems to create a mentality of 'I'd better buy it now because it won't be available later'. It also, of course, feels like a permanent link with the author; a memento of them actually meeting you.

A writer who attended my workshop, John Enright (author of the novel *New Jerusalem News,* 2015), told me a story about attending a festival to which he had brought along a simple selection of merchandise, as well as his books. He quickly realised that people didn't want the books so much because they wanted to order them online (many people prefer this, especially if they want e-Books or pristine copies as a gift for others), but they definitely wanted the merchandise! As his stocks of merchandise began to run out, John had to act quickly to create a competition so that everyone could have a fair chance of getting the products. What did they have to buy in order to have a chance of winning the merchandise? A book, of course!

Exercise

One of the reasons people like to buy books directly from the author is to have the books signed, either for themselves or to make the book an extra-special gift. Some writers are now creating personalised bookplates – an illustrated sticker about half the size of an average book page that can be stuck into the book – which they can sign and send out to fans. These could either be a free gift, as a nice gesture to your readers, or you could offer it as a low-cost piece of merchandise: fans can buy a signed bookplate directly from you, and you can dedicate and sign it according to their direction (for example, as a gift for someone). Many online sites offer personalised bookplate designs (e.g. www.bookplateink.com). You could even have a range that people can choose from, suited to different occasions.

12. Workshop time

If you'd like to warm up your little grey cells and think up merchandise ideas for a book before you start on your own work, then what follows are five different case studies. These were used with authors who attended the workshops I ran at the British Library and which eventually became this book.

Each one is a wholly imaginary book – although I'm claiming copyright in case I have inadvertently created some bestsellers! – in different genres and across both fiction and non-fiction. You may be tempted to just work on the genres closest to your heart, but thinking outside your genre can give you some interesting insights into what might and might not work for your own writing. Take ten minutes for each example and try to think up at least ten suitable items of merchandise for each. There's a list at the back of the book with ideas that were workshopped, but do try by yourself first, or with a friend. The results can be quite funny!

Romance: *Love's Flame*

Adam and Jenny were the perfect loving couple. But

somewhere along the way they lost the magic: working too hard, caught up in other things. It's only when Adam catches sight of Jenny's diary entry that he realises their relationship is on the rocks. Ending up in couples' counselling, their therapist sets them two tasks. One: communicate more often and more honestly. And two: recreate the six most important dates of their relationship. Adam and Jenny begin to write to one another via a diary, exploring their feelings, while the six dates bring up memories that might, just might, rekindle their love's flame.

WRITE IN YOUR MERCHANDISE IDEAS HERE:

1.

2.

3.

4.

5.

6.

7.

8.

9.

10.

Sci-Fi/Thriller: *A Child of Your Own*

In one moment, all across the globe, everyone is rendered infertile. In that one moment, children everywhere become a precious and valued commodity. At first, there are fights over the children already up for adoption, but when that source is used up almost overnight, every child becomes a target, as desperate would-be parents begin to look outside the legal system for a way to fulfil their last-ever chance of being a parent. Would your child be safe? Could you fight off the 'child-snatchers'? And what would it take for you to give up your child, when billionaires would offer you everything you ever dreamt of to take your child and raise it as their own?

WRITE IN YOUR MERCHANDISE IDEAS HERE:

1.

2.

3.

4.

5.

6.

7.

8.

9.

10.

Self-Help: *Making Every Minute Count*

Why is it that some people seem to have so much time available and get so much done in their lives, while the rest of us struggle to just get washed, dressed and out the door? In this new self-help book you'll find out how to:

- *Prioritise what you want to achieve*
- *Find every spare minute you have available within 24 hrs: whether you are commuting, breastfeeding, cooking, on your lunch break, at the hairdresser or even fast asleep!*
- *Make the very most of every single one of those minutes to achieve everything you thought was impossible.*

Ready to have more time, get more done and achieve your dreams? Start your stopwatches and hop on board.

WRITE IN YOUR MERCHANDISE IDEAS HERE:

1.

2.

3.

4.

5.

6.

7.

8.

9.

10.

Memoir: Picking the Grapes of Wrath

The Grapes of Wrath, *by John Steinbeck, is a classic of American literature, covering the 1930s Depression era in a combination of devastating honesty and poetic rage.* Picking The Grapes of Wrath *is a memoir by Mary Woodby and offers a child's view of the time. Following her itinerant family as they move from orchard to vineyard across California, picking fruit and trying desperately to make ends meet, seven-year-old Mary somehow makes a rough-and-ready childhood out of playing traditional games with the children in camps, a scrap of discarded wood carved into her only toy, and the taste of bruised fruit. Barely surviving the crushing blows of the Depression, Mary learns the skill of patchwork quilting from her hard-working mother and goes on to become one of America's most famous quilters.*

WRITE IN YOUR MERCHANDISE IDEAS HERE:

1.

2.

3.

4.

5.

6.

7.

8.

9.

10.

13. Good places to get merchandise made

There are more and more places you can go to have your products made and you should try out a few samples to see what you think of their quality and customer service before committing to them. Here are a few places I've either used myself or had writers recommend:

- Café Press (www.cafepress.com): offers lots of items you can personalise and sell online, similar to Zazzle. I haven't personally used it, but other writers have and tell me it is good.

- Etsy (www.etsy.com): features designer-makers (for collaborations), or if you have good craft skills on your own, then they are good for displaying your wares: jewellery, home decor, craft and fashion items.

- Harvey Maria (www.harveymaria.com): customised vinyl flooring.

- Redbubble (www.redbubble.com): good for t-shirts, stickers and more.

- Spoonflower (www.spoonflower.com): customised wallpaper, fabric, clothing patterns, gift-wrapping paper, even cloth posters for something a bit different.

- Vistaprint (www.vistaprint.co.uk): wide range of items based on photos/words: mugs, calendars, mouse mats, etc. Also good for your business needs (business cards, compliments slips, etc.).

- Woven Monkey (www.wovenmonkey.com): customised fabric.

- Zazzle (www.zazzle.co.uk): a huge range of merchandise for artists, a very simple set-up, and straightforward royalties. Very similar to self-publishing on Amazon for those of you who do this. I've started using them and they are definitely user-friendly. Very much worth a look.

14. Business Plan Template

I highly recommend that you have your own business plan. It's for you, not to give to a bank, but it gives you a direction, a path to follow. I wrote a business plan the year I committed to writing full-time and suddenly a whole host of opportunities seemed to open up. I'm pretty sure it's because I had finally focused on what I wanted to achieve and was looking out for those opportunities rather than being unaware of them passing me by.

If you don't make a business plan then it can be hard to spot good opportunities when they present themselves, because you don't know whether your overall goals will be served. Without a business plan, it's also really easy to get caught up doing things that are not really your priorities, and since no one I know has enough time, that's a waste.

You can read any good business book to get a business plan template, but I thought it might be useful to have one to hand which has been written with authors in mind. I've also added a few notes, specifically relevant to merchandise, into each section.

It's good to write out your one-year plan, with a brief summary of longer-term goals at the bottom, and stick it on the wall. Then break it down every month into what you can do that month to get closer to this year's goals, and prepare the building blocks/foundations for the future.

Always ask yourself before doing something: *Is this achieving my goals?* Try to say 'no' to minor projects that are using up your precious time for little reward. Read *The One Thing* (2014) by Gary Keller and Jay Papasan, if you need help in prioritising, but in essence it boils down to: what ONE thing is going to make the biggest difference? For example, I can go and write a bunch of Tweets, update my Facebook status etc. and kid myself that this is good because I am developing my online platform. But the reality is that if I only have an hour available – or even less – then really the biggest difference I can make to my goals is to crack on with my book in progress, which is not far off being finished, or complete the application for a Creative Writing Ph.D., which is an important part of my writing career's building blocks. Either of these is actually going to have a much bigger impact on my writing career overall, so I ought to focus on those.

Here are the headings you are going to use:

- The Goal, and how you get there
- Who and what do you want to be?
- Your marketplace and competition

- What do you have and what do you need?

- How much money do you need and how are you going to make it?

- How much time do you have?

- Who is going to help you?

- Risks and how to manage them

- Making yourself visible: Platform and marketing

The Goal and how you get there

You write this at the end because it's a summary of everything else. This section is usually called an 'executive summary', because it just sums up what you'll be doing as a reminder. It's a really good idea to turn this into a one-page summary you can have pinned up in front of you. I'm a fairly visual person so mine is just four shapes with the key points I need to remember:

My big overall goal (in a square): to be a full-time author making a good income. The way I do this is through three circles:

- Publish: i.e. get the books out there because they are my main product.

- Platform: get known.

- Profit: bring in multiple sources of income so that I'm not reliant on just one thing, also because I like doing things like developing products and teaching, as well as writing.

That's my big page. If I'm not doing one of those three

things then I'm wasting my time. Then I have details on all of those elements, with exactly what I mean for each one – targets etc. – but this is the page that keeps me on track. Simple words like 'full-time' mean something very specific to me that might be different to you, even if we used the same word. That's okay as long as we know what it means for ourselves.

Timings-wise, think 1 year, 3 years and 5 years ahead. You can also, of course, have a really long-term goal that you believe will take a long time to reach. For each target, break it down a bit, especially the coming year's targets. Work out what you need to do to achieve those goals.

- If I say I want to get three commissions for my writing then I need to sign up to the right newsletters that will alert me to opportunities, I need a good CV; I need some interesting ideas I could develop further; I need to write frequent and compelling pitches.

- If I say I want to do a writing qualification then I need to find out what's available and where; figure out how to fund it and what time commitment is required; make applications (time-consuming); and find some good referees to give me references, and so on.

Once you've filled in all the other sections, come back and create a one-page summary that reminds you of what you are trying to do.

What and who do you want to be?

What and who are you? Can you summarise who you are as a writer and where you want to get to as briefly as possible? It's a good thing to try, although trickier than it sounds.

Spend some time brainstorming around this. What do you want and when do you want it by? Find the core themes and what matters most to you and prioritise those. One writer might want to hone their writing skills over the next year, whereas another might want to increase their output and visibility. Another might want to ease off on their usual writing a little and bring in new elements: teaching; trying out a new genre; taking time to research a new historical series. Do you want to make writing your full-time job? And if so, how will you make enough money to live on?

You need to know what you are trying to achieve so that you can focus your attention on what really matters. If you feel you need to hone your writing skills, for example, then it would make sense to work with an editor, read some books on the craft, as well as the masters of your genre, take a few classes, develop a daily writing habit, and so on. Knowing the steps you need to go through is also useful because it should make you take each step seriously. I've met writers who hurry to submit their first draft to a literary agent, because they so badly want one, without doing what they really ought to do, which is making sure their work is of the highest possible quality first.

Bear in mind that your goals may also include other aspects of your life, not just your writing. When I decided to be a full-time author, I knew that what that actually meant was being a stay-at-home mother to my two small children until they both went to school full-time, when I would *really* be a full-time author rather than squeezing the writing around the kids. I also knew that this gave me a few years' grace to build up my writing career, which is why I signed on for a Creative Writing Ph.D., which will nicely finish just as both my kids enter full-time education. I want the freedom to travel and manage my own time, and this also contributed to committing to a writing career.

Now that you have thought about who you are and where you want to go, do a little audit. How far have you got to go? What are all the steps between here and there? Don't be discouraged by there being a lot: it's a good sign that you've thought things through properly, and also means you're breaking things down into manageable chunks.

When do things need to happen by? This year? 3 years? 5 years? Break it down into baby steps but keep your eyes on the overall goal. Think about all aspects: merchandise, genres, publishing styles, speaking, teaching etc. What is your mission, your vision, your purpose? What do you want to be known for? What do you want to give to the world? How much money do you really need to make? Don't be ignorant or embarrassed about this, there is a both a bottom line and a limitless number.

It may be worth creating a writing CV because it often shows up pretty quickly both what you have achieved and where the gaps are. How many books per year are you going to write? What are your goals for the books in terms of sales, merchandise, media coverage, reviews? Be specific but not verbose about it. Think about developing a portfolio of roles and income streams, because that's how most writers make enough money. It's pretty rare for a writer to make all their income just from book sales. What other work would you enjoy doing? I love to speak/teach, so I am happy developing that aspect of my portfolio. You might want to create a part-time or day job that enhances or makes use of your writing or love of books, such as copywriting or journalism, working to improve literacy or other roles.

Your marketplace and competition

You need to understand the marketplace you are in, and who your readers are. Some writers are truly offended when you refer to their books as 'products'. All I can say is that a book can be a work of art *and* a product. If you want to take an entrepreneurial approach to your writing career then you simply can't be offended about this issue.

You need to research the area in which you are writing – you may have more than one of course. Analyse the genre, style, audience, length of books, cover styles and more. Look at similar authors in your area – or those you really admire – and consider how they market themselves; what their websites look like; what their goals seem to be; how they communicate and on what platforms; if they have merchandise; who publishes them or if they are indie (self-published), etc. The more you know about the market you are in, the better you can operate in it and make your readers happy by finding them, offering them a product they will love and communicating positively with them.

Think carefully about your customers. Who are they and what do they want from you? Help? Enjoyment? Escape? Chills and thrills? Check the words positive reviewers use to see what your role is in relation to them. I did a 'word cloud' for my historical novel from the five-star reviews and found that *enjoyment* was a key word, along with words that indicated my readers enjoyed the clothes, food, history and relationships in my story. It gave me a very good insight into what my ideal reader wants from my novels. Luckily, it seems to be what I want to give them!

Where can you find your ideal reader and what else do they read? What kind of merchandise do you think they would like?

What do you have and what do you need?

Now that you are getting an idea of what you want to be and what you want to achieve, you need to work out what you already have and what you need in order to get there.

What do you already have? A good writing habit, a website, a computer or laptop, a publishing deal, an agent? Enough time and money to write? Professional contacts? You may have all or none of these, but identify everything you do have, and think about how to make the most of it.

You will also need to identify what you *don't* have and need to work on, or prioritise: more books to your name, better visibility (platform), more time to write, more money, a better understanding of how to use social media etc.

For your merchandise: what do you want to make and how is that going to get done? Do you need money, skills, a collaborator? What do you already have that could make it easier?

Once you are clear on what you have and what you need, work out how to make the most of what you have and how to get what you need. It may take a while, but work away at improving your situation.

How much money do you need and how are you going to make it?

People are shy about this. They come up with vague answers: authors are badly paid, and so on. That doesn't answer the question: 'How much do *you* actually need to live on?' Sit down and work it out. That's your minimum. How much would you like to make? This question is even worse as most people either say 'oh, you know… wouldn't it be fun to be a millionaire', or else are certain they can't make their minimum, let alone a maximum amount. This is not a good way to think.

Write down your minimum. Now write down how much you would really and truly like to make: perhaps in stages. You might say right now you want to work towards the minimum so that you can be a full-time author, then you would like to earn 10% more a year later, and so on. And now, what are you willing to do to achieve this? You may need to put in some serious extra hours. You may need to downsize your lifestyle to be able to commit to the full-time writing that will eventually allow you to make more money. You may wish to find a day job that you enjoy, and that complements your writing.

If you have any issues around money – a *lot* of people do – then I'd suggest reading *Get Rich, Lucky Bitch* (2013) by Denise Duffield-Thomas, which is a rude, funny but true look at some of the money issues many people have, and which has some good exercises to read through so you can try and get rid of bad money habits and attitudes. I did this when I decided to be a full-time author instead of someone's employee, because I didn't want to have anything holding me back.

The average author income is apparently around about £9,000 and falling. One year in, I hit £14,000 and secured that for three years ahead of me. I'm not boasting because I still have a very long way to go, but you have to think creatively about how you are going to make money as an author and not take the average as your benchmark. Take it as something to trample on.

Be business-like about money:

- Your merchandise *must* be profitable or they're just gifts.

- Set up some financial tracking for your writing: money in; money out.

- Be honest and clear with the tax people.

- Create an invoice template.

- Expect to be paid. This is a *big* debate in the writing industry right now and I would like all authors to consider this point: if you are not going to be paid then: 1) why not? it's worth questioning; and 2) what *are* you going to get out of it, and is it worth the money you are *not* going to be making?

- Don't be fobbed off too easily with 'visibility' as payment. I once got an almost full-page feature spread in the *Evening Standard* newspaper with a hugely positive review of my book. Their 1.7m readers were the book's absolutely perfect target audience. Sales peak as a response? 12 books. Visibility does not necessarily pay the bills! I was glad of the review but also pleased I didn't give up any unpaid time to it.

How much time do you have and what has to get done?

You know what needs to be done. How are you going to squeeze in the time? If you're a full-time writer then you are very lucky, but make sure you are actually making the most of that time. Are you stretching yourself? Or has the Internet swallowed half your day? Author RJ Ellory is my inspiration here: the man gets an amazing amount of work done, from writing to events to communicating with fans. If you ever hear him speak at a conference, I guarantee you'll sit there with your mouth open if he tells you about what he gets done in a day, let alone a week or more.

Remember to prioritise the most important things; the ones that will make the biggest difference. For example, developing merchandise is great – obviously, I would think that! – but don't get swept away with it and forget to write the books! To start with, keep it simple, until you are sure it is paying for the time you are investing in it.

If you don't have a lot of time… welcome to the club! There are so many, many superstar writers who started out in this position, rising at appalling hours, scribbling in their lunch breaks, and so on. You can do the same.

Here are a few ways to get some extra time: bear in mind that even 30 minutes a day adds up to 3.5 hrs a week, and that's actually a fair amount of extra time you can devote to your writing. If I told you I could give you an extra half-writing day every week you'd probably be pleased. Although often, limited time can actually help you to concentrate better!

- Get up early
- Go to bed late
- Write while kids nap

- Write on your commute to work

- Get into work an hour early so you can devote that additional time to writing

- Write during your lunch hour

- Write while breastfeeding (I wrote a whole book doing this)

- Cut down on the Internet and TV: they both use up a lot of time and it's not always to your best advantage. Or use a tablet or laptop while others are watching TV so you can all be together (children excel at using several screens at the same time)

- Investigate different ways of working: can you dictate your work onto software such as Dragon? Some writers love this. Can you collaborate with another writer? Can you speed up your typing from two fingers to ten by learning to touch-type?

- If you love your social media and need to keep it going to build your online presence then use something like Hootsuite (www.Hootsuite. com) to schedule your messages to the big wide world. Little-bitty work often takes up more time than the same work done as a big block.

Set yourself some scary targets and see if your output speeds up. Try things like NaNoWriMo (www.nanowrimo. com), where you write a book In a month. Sometimes work takes the amount of time we have available. I'm very guilty of this: the less amount of time I have, the quicker the work will get done. Try it!

Who is going to help you?

In this section you write down all the help you need – time, resources, moral support, professional services etc. – and where it's going to come from.

You're going to need some help. Your kids will need to let you work while they play sometimes. Your partner could let you get in an extra half-hour's writing time without moaning about doing the washing-up. Your friends will have to excuse you not going out once in a while so you can meet your targets. You are blessed if those around you are supportive of what you do. If they are not, then you need to be firm and find ways to compromise that still allow you to do what you need to do, but get people on board who are dragging their feet. Make a list of how those around you could support you.

Look out for mentors. These can be real-life or virtual. My virtual mentor is Joanna Penn (www.thecreativepenn. com), because despite never having met her in person I've learnt so very much from her already and find her inspirational as a writer-entrepreneur. It makes me happy when she achieves her goals because some of them are my future goals, and it makes me feel they are possible, so I mentally cheer her on. Mentors can inspire you without even knowing it. Look out for ways to get moral support and tips: from online writing communities, writing groups, reading good books for writers, and so on.

You'll need some professional help: maybe book designers, editors, a literary agent, childcare, accountant, and so on. Use recommended contacts wherever possible and surround yourself with the best, even if it takes a while to find them, or you have to upgrade a few times. Don't do things that you're not good at unless you're going to learn to do them really well. I could learn to format my own books but you know what? I like to write, I don't have much time and I have the loveliest book designers in the world. I'd rather write and let them do the work they do so well. Becoming a member of the Society of Authors (www.societyofauthors. org), the Alliance of Independent Authors (www. allianceindependentauthors.org), or associations within your genre can be an important step in acknowledging your own professional status and intentions.

For your merchandise: which designers, manufacturers and other suppliers do you need on board? Do you have contacts already, or do you need to go and do some research?

Don't forget general cheerleaders: I have a few people in my life who are ludicrously, wonderfully supportive. They are my cheerleaders and they go crazy when I am successful. When it's not going so well, they paint a rosy future for me so I get back up on my feet and keep going. Everyone needs some cheerleaders. Know who they are and love them lots.

Risks and how to manage them

Life is rarely all plain sailing, even if you're an optimist. Think about risks to your plan and work out some contingencies. Here are a few to start you off:

- Back up your work, then if your computer fails you'll only cry a bit, not a lot.

- Have plans in place if your childcare fails. I have about five different childminders I and my children know well by now, just in case my usual carers are on holiday, or can't cover a different day when I unexpectedly need to work.

- How do you deal with procrastination, spending hours watching cats on the internet instead of writing, creative blocks etc.? Find some good solutions that work for you. Perhaps physical exercise or working on something different; setting extreme targets; or taking a proper break?

- What will happen to your income if one of your income streams fails/disappears? What if the magazine you always write for changes editor and they don't want to know? What if your publisher drops you? I've seen many of these stories happen to writers I know.

- What happens if your supplier for merchandise stops the collaboration or turns out a shoddy product?

- What if you fall ill?

- Etc.

You get the picture. Make a risk list and figure out how to overcome each risk. It's boring and a little bit scary, but important and worthwhile.

Making yourself visible: Platform and marketing

People go on about 'platform' for authors and it took me a while to really grasp what on earth they were talking about. It just means *how visible you are.* When you write, are there 25,000 people ready to buy your books or are there 100?

Start by reading a few good books on this: *Create your Writer Platform* by Chuck Sambuchino, *Sell your book like Wildfire!* by Rob Eagar, *How to Market Books* by Alison Baverstock, and *How to Market a Book* by Joanna Penn are all great reads (see Resources), and will give you tonnes of good ideas, both for your general platform and also for marketing specific books – and a lot of their marketing advice applies to merchandise too.

Assess where you are at with your platform. For starters, do you have your own website hosted on your own domain name, and which you can reasonably easily update? Does it look professional and interesting? Do you have something that brands you? I chose to have a professional calligrapher write my name for me and it now acts as my logo.

You need to be professional to be treated like a professional. Get a good photo of yourself done and a business card. I've had professional photo shoots done and each one cost me less than £20 because I looked out for deals on sites like Groupon: you can get a photo session where they do your hair and make-up and you get one really nice shot. It's a total bargain and you will look great.

I've had people look at me dubiously when I say I'm a writer. I get out a business card that says 'writer' on it and suddenly they're treating me differently, as though I've suddenly become a *real* writer in front of their very eyes. I find this quite funny but it also means I've learnt to always carry my business cards. A smart business card is very cheap. I use Vistaprint (www.vistaprint.com) but there are plenty of other sites.

Decide which social-media platforms you are willing and able to work on. Unless you are a fantastically good user and have a lot of time I'd suggest two would be enough to start with. For example, there is little point in choosing Twitter if you hate it, except that I have noticed that journalists seem to really, really like it and will use it even when there are quicker ways of contacting you, which is worth knowing.

A lot of writers now focus on developing an email list of their fans, by offering what Nick Stephenson (www. blog. yourfirst10kreaders.com) calls 'Reader Magnets': you offer something for free (like a book) in return for their email address. You can start with the email list manager Mail Chimp (www.mailchimp. com), which is free up to 2,000 names on your list.

How will your merchandise fit into your marketing? What role do you want it to play? How high up the priority list is it? If it's not high, then either wait a little or do some toe-dipping to start you off. Remember the flowering tea balls in the palanquin favour box? That took about half an hour's research on Amazon to see what was available and a very small outlay (well under £100) to make up the first batch. Experiment!

Draw up a simple marketing plan: how to market yourself (this might include branding, a photo and a business card); how to market your books overall (e.g. the email-marketing list); how to market each one individually (e.g. develop a product that matches your bestselling book).

Don't do everything straight away or you'll drop dead with exhaustion and get no writing done. Read the books, brainstorm where you are and where you want to be, and then prioritise: what will actually make the biggest difference to your visibility? Do that first. Also, learn to do the stuff that you're going to need on an ongoing basis. I put aside a whole lot of smaller projects for almost a year while I wrote a novella so that I could set up an email-marketing list with a reader magnet in place. I learnt to use Wordpress because I wanted control over updating my own site. Use Hootsuite to keep the social-media workload manageable.

Top Tip

Think about how you dress when you're going to be seen: it's part of your brand. I've met people who have a key colour they use on their website *and* in their clothing: e.g. a pink website header and a pink scarf, or a duck-egg blue business card and a duck-egg blue jacket. It might sound too much, but you know what…? It makes them instantly recognisable when you meet them or if you go hunting for them online.

Review the plan all the time!

Remember that key sixth step in the NPD diagram (p.61) on reviewing your products? You need to do the same with your business plan. To start with, you'll need to update it because as each year goes by you'll need to plan one more year ahead just to keep up. So an annual review is very important. But it's worth reviewing more often, especially if changes mean you're no longer up to date. This can happen in a number of ways:

1. The plan may need to change because it's been more successful than you ever dreamt of: you've smashed your targets and are loaded down with wonderful new opportunities. Brilliant! Update the plan, set even more amazing targets and go get 'em! Also, take a moment to congratulate yourself and to think about why it worked. Being objective about successes and failures is key to being more effective as you go on. Write down your key thoughts and store them somewhere you will be able to find them in the future.

2. The plan may need to change because something has altered: you may have found a whole new area

you hadn't thought of before (new genres, teaching/ speaking opportunities, etc.), or there may be shifts in your family life. Take a look at the plan and alter it accordingly: add new directions; find solutions; perhaps remove other elements that are no longer relevant or which are lower priority and you don't have time for etc.

3. Finally, the plan may need to change because you are not achieving your goals. If this happens you need to take a good hard look at yourself and the plan.

- Is it failing because you are not putting in the effort; for example, procrastinating or being too reticent about grabbing opportunities? Then you need to buck up!

- Or it may be that your targets were not realistic, and then you need to adjust the plan: goals should be stretching but not pie-in-the-sky dreaming.

- A third possibility is that the goals are being achieved, but more slowly than you thought. If that's the case then see if you can make them happen faster or whether you need to be more realistic with your timelines.

The important thing is that your plan should be up to date, all the time, because it should act as a guide for you. You should be able to glance through it and be inspired, reminded and remotivated to achieve your goals. It should alert you to opportunities that arise because you know they are right for you.

Good luck! I hope your hard work makes all your plans come true and that your business plan has to be updated *weekly* because of all the great things that are happening for you!

15. Possible merchandise

In case you got stuck earlier on, here are ten items of merchandise for each of the imaginary books I gave you to practice on (see Chapter 12). A big thank you to all the great workshop attendees who came up with many more suggestions than I was able to list here, but I have chosen some of your fun ones. Thanks for all the giggles!

Romance: *Love's Flame*

1. A couples' journal to write messages to one another in.

2. *Rekindle the Flame*; a non-fiction collaboration with a couples' therapist.

3. A 'date' calendar to remind couples to book in date nights.

4. A pack of fifty cards with fun, free date ideas.

5. Voucher for a Laughing Workshop.

6. DVD of body language for relationships.

7. Work-life balance masterclass.

8. An app that stores your favourite messages to each other and replays them if you need a lift.

9. Candles.

10. Run a competition: Tell me your six best dates and win an experience.

Sci-Fi: *A Child of Your Own*

1. Experience voucher: shooting range.

2. Experience voucher: martial arts.

3. Child tracking device.

4. Home-security products (alarms, CCTV etc.).

5. IVF charitable products.

6. Video game: Protecting children.

7. Matching adult/child t-shirts.

8. Child safety app.

9. Children's reins for toddlers to keep them safe.

10. Safety board game for children to learn things like their full name, address, parents' names, phone number, emergency service contacts etc.

Self-Help: *Making Every Minute Count*

1. Calendar with reminders of how to find time in your life.

2. The 'to do list' diary.

3. Vouchers for meal-solution providers (e.g. meals delivered to your house).

4. The Priority Poster: A daily reminder of what matters most to you.

5. Clocks in all shapes and sizes, physical and as apps, including stopwatches and egg timers.

6. A daily wristband to focus you on the day's priorities (e.g. Monday is fitness; Tuesday is family...).

7. A YouTube testimonials site so you can be inspired by others.

8. A 1-2-1 phone session with the author to discuss your own personal situation: This would be charged quite highly.

9. Cups with motivational messages.

10. Aromatherapy products to make you energetic and focused.

Memoir: *Picking The Grapes of Wrath*

1. Non-fiction book on how to quilt.

2. Quilting kit to make a patchwork quilt for a child.

3. Wooden toy range from the era.

4. Posters from the era.

5. Cards with recipes from the era.

6. Bookmarks with Mary's grandmother's favourite sayings.

7. Experience voucher: How to carve wooden toys.

8. Experience voucher: Picking grapes in a vineyard.

9. Customised fabric design available to buy on Spoonflower.

10. Print of Mary and her family: their only family photograph.

16. Sixty items to turn into merchandise

1. Jewellery
2. Cards (playing)
3. Cards (greeting)
4. Board games
5. Apps and software
6. Calendars (think historical, sci-fi etc.)
7. Journals/notepads
8. Non-fiction books to accompany fiction and vice versa
9. Colouring books
10. Figurines
11. Artwork (if illustrator), or posters with words/poems/extracts etc.
12. Umbrellas
13. Passport holders
14. Luggage and shopping bags, purses, toiletries bags, bags to carry yoga kit in
15. Toys

16. Clothing (beautiful/fashionable): sleepwear (think of sexy pyjama sets for erotica from Spoonflower), yoga clothing sets, ties, caps, hats, t-shirts etc. Don't skimp on the quality of cotton

17. Tea towels

18. Bookmarks, keyrings and other trinkets

19. USB sticks

20. Pens, pencils, colouring pens, chalks, crayons, paints

21. Guitar picks (Zazzle)

22. Food and drink products

23. Activity books for kids (or grown-ups!)

24. Wrapping paper (Spoonflower) and other gift stationery (e.g. gift bags, writing paper)

25. Wedding-related items; e.g. favours or invitations

26. Photo albums

27. Cookbooks

28. Kitchenware, including crockery, coffee mugs, coasters (try offices, bars, clubs, cafés as outlets, as well)

29. Stickers, including wall stickers (decals)

30. CDs of music

31. Telephones for the home in interesting shapes, or vintage styles

32. Covers for Kindles, iPhones, tablets, laptops etc.

33. Serving trays

34. Furniture

35. Decorative home accessories (e.g. clocks, mirrors, candleholders, cushions)

36. Kits for making something (craft-like); e.g. shoes, hats, rag rugs etc.

37. DIY Voucher books, where people write in tasks they will do for one another, such as a massage from a partner, or your kids doing the chores

38. Duvet covers or throws

39. Gardening items

40. Naming something, like a star or rose

41. Perfume or toiletries

42. Baby clothing and accessories, like dummies

43. Sports products like balls, yoga mats, ping-pong bats (Zazzle), and so on

44. Fitness products: clothing, equipment, water bottles etc.

45. Business gifts (everything from coffee mugs to stress balls, mouse pads to hampers)

46. Experiences (like Red Letter Days)

47. Fridge magnets; e.g. for kids or to hold up photos and recipes

48. Car magnets/stickers or licence plate covers

49. Personalised fabric (Spoonflower and Woven Monkey): would be wonderful for craft people, kids, fashionistas etc.

50. Custom wallpaper (Spoonflower)

51. Customised clothing patterns: you are sent printed fabric plus the pattern, so that you can make your own clothes, handbags etc.

52. Fabric posters, for something a bit different (Spoonflower)

53. Customised vinyl flooring (Harvey Maria)

54. Bandanas

55. Sunglasses (Zazzle)

56. Special top-end editions of your books with amazing binding etc. for collectors (this goes down very well; e.g. as Kickstarter gifts)

57. Travel card/ticket holders

58. Badges/pins

59. Wristbands

60. Post-it notes

17. And finally...

Good luck! I hope this book inspires you to create some really fun merchandise. Do write and tell me all about it; I'd love to know what you develop: Melissa@melissaaddey.com

Remember to make it both fun and profitable and you'll have a ball!

Resources

What follows is a combination of books and websites, including author websites, that you might find useful as you develop your merchandise and general entrepreneurial spirit as a writer. Many of the sites focus on indie (self-published) authors, but traditionally published authors can use their ideas too. Indie authors tend to be a very entrepreneurial breed and also very supportive. I've put a little bit of information about each. All of these have stood me in good stead over the past years.

Books:

Baverstock, Alison, *How to Market Books*, 2015, 5th edition, Routledge.
This book is very comprehensive and has been updated and revised to take the social-media age into account. It covers a multitude of situations, from book covers to literary events, and includes some good examples of real-life marketing plans for books.

Duffield-Thomas, Denise, *Get Rich, Lucky Bitch,* 2013, CreateSpace.
I recommend reading this book before tackling the financial aspects of your business plan. Read the book, do the exercises and focus on earning the money you want, whether through your books, merchandise or anything else.

Eagar, Rob, *Sell your book like Wildfire!* 2012, Writer's Digest Books.
Contains lots of good ideas for marketing your books. Many of the ideas would work for merchandise too. Includes both fiction and non-fiction case studies.

Keller, Gary, and Papasan, Jay, *The One Thing,* 2014, John Murray Learning.
This book helps you prioritise what will make the biggest difference to achieving your goals by making you focus on one thing. Very useful when you have limited time and big goals!

Penn, Joanna, *How to Make a Living with your Writing*, 2015, CreateSpace.
A book to make you think about many different ways in which your writing can make you a real income.

Penn, Joanna, *Business for Authors*, 2014, CreateSpace.
A good guide to becoming a professional author.

Penn, Joanna, *How to Market a Book*, 2013, CreateSpace.
Lots of practical tips for marketing your book, especially as an indie author.

Sambuchino, Chuck, *Create your Writer Platform,* 2012, Writer's Digest Books.
This book explains 'platform' very well and has a lot of good advice on how to develop your own as a writer, covering both fiction and non-fiction.

Business Advice

The British Library's Business & IP Centre www.bl.uk/ business-and-ip-centre
The Centre is a wonderful resource for entrepreneurs and can help with everything from one-to-one advice on developing new products to providing market reports and answering copyright queries.

Merchandise providers (details of each in Chapter 13)

Café Press (www.cafepress.com)
Etsy (www.etsy.com)
Harvey Maria (www.harveymaria.com)
Redbubble (www.redbubble.com)
Spoonflower (www.spoonflower.com)
Vistaprint (www.vistaprint.co.uk)
Woven Monkey (www.wovenmonkey.com)
Zazzle (www.zazzle.co.uk)

Websites:

Alliance of Independent Authors www.allianceindependentauthors.org
Contains a lot of good advice and interesting ideas for marketing books, developing good writing practices and all aspects of self-publishing.

Funds for Writers www.fundsforwriters.com
Hope Clark's highly recommended Funds for Writers newsletter lists grants, fellowships, residencies, markets to write for and includes brief articles with a lot of good advice. It's free although the subscription version is a very reasonable price too and worth investing in if you find the free version useful.

Society of Authors www.societyofauthors.org
An important organisation to be part of, offering advice and support to writers at different stages of their careers.

The Creative Penn www.thecreativepenn.com
Joanna Penn's great website has huge amounts of good entrepreneurial and writing advice for authors. Her books are also very helpful for those wanting to make their writing into a business (see Books section above).

Your first 10k Readers www.blog.yourfirst10kreaders.com
Nick Stephenson focuses on marketing books by developing an email list of committed readers, which would also help enormously with selling your merchandise. There are lots of free videos and a free e-Book you can download, called 'Reader Magnets', on his website. Have a look at them all. I can also recommend his paid course, which goes into a lot more detail and has a very positive and supportive private Facebook community attached to it.

Winskill Editorial www.winskilleditorial.co.uk
A professional editing service, very useful for general writing but also in case your merchandise involves text.

30988715R00083

Printed in Great Britain
by Amazon